BISHOP G.M. BOONE

"THIS IS MY STORY"

"THIS IS MY STORY"

Written by:

BISHOP G.M. BOONE

INTERVIEWED AT THE AGE OF 94 YEARS OLD FOR THIS BOOK.

Let the Life I've lived and the Service I've given,
Speak for me.

COPYRIGHT

Library of Congress Cataloging-In-Publication Data

ISBN 978-0-692-46391-8

Book designed by: Mrs. Chiquitta Harris
Editor: Dr. Dorma Jeane McGruder

DEDICATION

This book is dedicated to my partner in life, love, marriage, labor and ministry, my lovely wife Mae Dee 'Mary' Boone. Without you working by my side and sacrificing every step of the way, our family, church, organization and this book - would never have been possible. Thank you for your love, support and for turning every house into a home.

ACKNOWLEDGMENTS

*Some of the people who
influenced my life the most.*

My Father, Mr. Shepherd Boone

My Mother, Mother Fielda Boone

Brother O.B. Barnes

District Elder Rush L. Lockhart, Sr.

Bishop Heardie Leaston

Bishop Willie Lee

Mother Louella Heard

Evangelist Helen Glenn

Dr. Lovora J. Walker

Dr. Shirley Ann Moore

TABLE OF CONTENTS

FOREWORD

by

MAE DEE 'MARY' BOONE

Growing up in Oxford, Mississippi, only God knew what He had in store for me. As the daughter of an Apostolic Preacher, there were two rules that I was aware of very early and they were 1. My Daddy was very much in charge and I was expected to be obedient. 2. I would marry someone who is saved - baptized in the Name of the Lord Jesus Christ and filled with the gift of the Holy Ghost. In regards to the second rule, God sent me one of the greatest blessings I could ever have right to my doorstep in the person of my husband who was then Brother, now Bishop G.M. Boone. At that initial conversation over seven decades ago, we had no way of knowing the journey that would bring us to 2015.

Only God knew that we needed one another to walk this road. I'm so thankful that The Lord has successfully led us through 69 years of marriage, allowed us to raise six children, elevated him from Assistant Pastor to establishing New Liberty Apostolic Faith Church and then to Presiding Bishop of the Apostolic Assemblies of Christ.

Only God knew the grace I would need to stand by his side all of these years. The world sees, knows, loves and serves him as Pastor, Bishop, Presiding Bishop and Founder. I however see, know, love and serve him as my best friend and husband. God gave me a man who knows, loves and serves Him.

Only God knew how to pour into my husband when he was just a little boy what he would need when we got married. God made him into a husband, father, grandfather, provider, leader, confidante, advisor, entrepreneur, teacher and friend. God equipped him with all the things my children and I would need by giving him the determination, ability and skill to make the decisions that were right for us.

Only God knew what man to pick to bless my children with an excellent father. He has taught our children and demonstrated to our grandchildren and our great-grandchildren how to work hard and be responsible and give nothing less than their best in all that they do.

Only God knew what leader to place at the head of the New Liberty Apostolic Faith Church. He has always taught holiness with wisdom, love, patience, understanding and strength and because of his love for God's people and his heart and zeal for souls, New Liberty continues to grow.

Only God knew the angry waves that would come as the Apostolic Assemblies of Christ moved forward and began to grim. Thankfully, God planted in my husband the ability to lay a strong foundation that will keep the Apostolic Assemblies of Christ standing in the decades ahead.

Only God knew how to give me the honor of being the wife and best friend to the man I have always depended on for provision, turned to in times of struggle, leaned on in the storm and enjoyed blessings when the sun was shining. He gave me a man that after 69 years of marriage, I am still proud to say that I am the wife of the one and only Bishop G.M. Boone.

PROLOGUE

After 95 years of life, I certainly have a lot to talk about and I won't be able to share it all here, but I will start by saying that I thank God for what He has done. He has allowed me to successfully navigate through the responsibilities and challenges of pastoring a great Church, leading a thriving organization and most of all raising my beautiful family.

My hope is that this book will cause someone to see what they can do when they make up their mind, whether it is in their home, job or even in their relationship with Christ. I pray that someone will come to realize through my story that while salvation is a requirement, it is also the only walk of life that is as sweet, life-changing and rewarding.

Join me on this journey as I share with you, my story.

CHAPTER 1

CHILDHOOD MEMORIES & CHILDHOOD STORIES

Alright I'm entering into my life story.

They say I was born May 31, 1920 in Myrtle, Mississippi.

Coming into this life I was told that I was a sickly little baby. The doctor recommended that I drink warm cow milk for six or eight weeks. Get as much of it in me as possible. My mother saw to that happening and the name of the cow was Lil. She was a Holstein cow, a milk cow, she wasn't the butter cow but she was the one that gave a lot of milk and so that's what they said began to heal my sickness. Leaving from there I came on into life as a little weakly sickly boy but God began to strengthen me.

Daddy & Mama

I got along very, very well with my mama and daddy. It was a lovely relationship. Both of them were jewels. My mother loved me. My daddy loved me. They both were School teachers. They treated me very well. Sometimes we thought the discipline and what they said didn't make sense and sometimes they jacked you up but in the end, I guess it worked. I had 12 sisters, I was right in the middle with six beneath and six above. As I came on up with my older sisters, the six that were above me I was familiar with them and of course the younger siblings came later and as every one of them came in I accepted them graciously as part of the family.

My mother's parents were Millie and Marshall Coleman and they loved me. I was only between 5 and 9 years old when they died but I remember their love. I remember an incident between granddaddy and daddy that still stays with me now.

Granddaddy & Grandmama Coleman

Granddaddy Marshall

Granddaddy and daddy were always competing. They were talking about shooting daddy's double barrel shotgun and granddaddy said he was faster than daddy.

"I can shoot it faster than you can."

"I don't think you can. I'm faster than you are."

But what happened was that my granddaddy put two fingers on each trigger, and as soon as he pulled one he pulled the other one at the same time and shot the gun. My daddy took one finger and pulled just one trigger then put one finger on the other trigger and pulled that. Granddaddy Marshall did shoot it faster. I remember that.

I began to think about how the Lord Himself how that He embraced me and supported me through the struggle of life being one of the young black men that was raised up in the south, down in the State of Mississippi, where it was known as one of the most prejudiced states in the nation.

That is where I came up. I came up through hard times. During that time my daddy and the work force were down, and they were hard times. I came up through the depression where it was hard to find anything to do. Wasn't no such thing as going and finding a job saying jobs was out there and all of that. But my daddy being a schoolteacher, he was able to make ends meet to carry us on until we got just a little further over in life.

When I was around five years old it was a thing then, that if mama and daddy went to the store that the child would always look for a little piece of candy or something. But I remember my daddy went to the store and when he went he had just a little bit of money. So in taking that little money he spent out and I couldn't get any candy, I couldn't get anything. And as a caring and a sharing father, he stopped along the road side while we were walking back home, opened a bag of sugar, told me to open my hand, he poured some sugar in my hand for me to eat that sugar because I didn't get no candy. That made a great impression upon me. It made me even feel that some of my children benefited just from that act of my father. Of course from that standpoint it was hard times, hard times, hard times.

One of the great things I remember in life after I got around five years old was my mother. She was a very favorable, faithful mother working hard and doing all that she could do and of course she had a habit of dipping snuff. This snuff dipping was a thing that if you ran out it was almost like putting a spell on a person. And anytime my mother ran out of snuff the cats, the dogs, the chickens and everything around her knew mama was out of snuff. So it created something in my mind that I didn't want to see her out of snuff. So as God would have it I could find money, I would find a penny here, a penny there and I began to save those pennies purposely just for one reason. If mama was out of snuff I would buy her a nickel box of snuff.

And this is how I would maintain that money. I would put it in one of her old snuff boxes, take it and put it up in the smokehouse, up on the ceiling where the other children would not know where it was. Nobody would

Mama

know where it was but me. Then when she was out of snuff, I would get that nickel and get her a box of snuff. I found that created something in my mind to kind of visualize, anticipate and prepare for what was ahead. I maintained that and I thank God for it today because it gave me somewhat of a vision. And from that point on I began to start working.

My daddy started me to plowing when I was five years old. Daddy's mules names were Tiger and Tuck. He showed me how to handle the mules and gave me good, clear instructions.

"Don't turn the mules a loose. If you turn them a loose they will get away."

But at five years old, at that same time I took hold of those words from my daddy. I had the tenacity to hold on to them under any circumstances. Just a few short weeks after that when I was plowing, something came up and scared the mules and I remember them, dragging me, plow and all, all the way across the field but I was determined not to turn them a loose. My daddy's words encouraged me to stay behind them and try harder. When my daddy got to me, I was still holding on to the mules. He complimented me for that and told me what he saw.

"You are going to be a man if you keep that up."

I grabbed that as another thing to substantiate me and reinforced that within myself.

"I'm going to be a man."

"I'm going to hold to that."

"I'm going to make my daddy proud."

"I am going to be the young man that he wants me to be."

I kept on plowing that day and did not stop. I broke them in and made them plow harder. We worked, and we worked, and we worked. From there I began to work, cutting the wood, doing all the work that my daddy did. Anything that he did I was a part of it. He had a way of encouraging me after I was about six or seven years old.

"You are a young man now."

Then I started trying to walk like a man.

Talk like a man.

Act like a man.

Do things like men.

I thank God for it even today! Life has always been a challenge to me. I always felt that if my daddy did it, I can do it. Thank God. That is the way I feel today.

That is why I encourage these young men today, and instill in them to be a man, you come here a boy and grow into a man. Be a good man.

In 1887 daddy, Shepherd Boone graduated from Mississippi Normal School in Holly Springs, Mississippi and went on to receive his Teaching Certificate from the State of Mississippi. During the summer months, my father taught school on a college level at Rust College in Holly Springs, Mississippi.

As I reminisce I think about my school days. At the time that we were going to school, the school was Lebanon Chapel there in Oxford, Mississippi a rural school. At that particular time daddy was a teacher. And of course being hard times and always trying to help provide and bring in something to eat, I played hooky from school and went hunting that day. I never will forget the time when my daddy slapped me so very hard. I was surprised and disappointed in it but he did it. He slapped me and then asked questions.

"Where have you been?"

"I went hunting."

"Why didn't you tell me?"

And about that time he slapped me. I felt so bad because I got out and I had about two rabbits, maybe one squirrel to add to our meal. I called myself helping provide something. I was kind of disappointed but after all I had a good daddy. But I think about it now and I reminisce about it and I appreciate it, but at the same time those were the things that were helping me to try and bring in food for everybody to help add to what daddy was doing to support our family. We were eating and needed to change our diet, because we had eaten up all the chickens that we could spare at that particular time, so I had to get out and get some rabbit, squirrel, possums, coons or something. I stayed out of school for that. But we laugh about that now.

There were other teachers I had during that time, going to the same school. Schooling was a thing back then for black people different than it is now. Most of us didn't have time for school. We didn't have the time to put in. We had to be cut off for gathering crops. If it wasn't our crops, we would go somewhere else to pick somebody else's cotton to bring some money in to do other things that we needed to do. We never did have the opportunity for school as we should have had. That made it pretty hard for some of the black people then in the heart of Mississippi.

I saw what my mother went through and I knew at that point, I was going to be a good husband. My mother's parents got sick, and she lost her mother and her father. At the time that they were down sick, she wanted to go to be with them where they lived in Chicago. Times were so hard that my dad could not even get the money, could not even borrow the money to send her to Chicago to stand by their bedside while they lived and took their last breath. She only needed $5.00 or $6.00 for the train ticket. I saw her walking through the house crying. I saw her laboring in her spirit with the hurt and she had to stand there and cry. It put something in my heart to this extent.

I made up my mind then and there, if I ever get a girl and get married, my wife will never go through this. I purposed in my heart and even though I was a child, I asked God to Guide my spirit. I will never act like that when I get to be a man.

I purposed in my heart and even though I was a child, I asked God to Guide my spirit.

I was six years old and saw a bow-legged pigeon toed five year old girl named Alberta Hill and said I was going to take care of her. She was one of our neighbor's, Mr. Ernest Hill's daughter. That is the girl I was going to marry as a six year old. I would lay in bed, figure out about how I was going to take care of her and I had a dream she would never go through what my mother went through in her married life.

And from that I feel that God was building my most holy faith and ambition so when the challenge came for me, when I got married I would know what to do. And for that cause I feel that He has been instrumental in my life. On through the years coming up as a teenager I set my mind like that.

The only thing I did not like about my childhood was that as a child coming up, times were so hard and everything was so hard to get your hands on to survive. I disliked it so much that I built up in my spirit a strong determination that made me vow to myself. "It will never be like that when I get to be a man." As I traveled on, I went on and later on we began to grow up in life.

At 12 years old, most of the prejudiced white people around there knew George even those that did not own stores. I remember at that time how I always was a person that had favor with the white man. I could go to those stores and tell them I wanted this, I wanted that, I wanted the other and I could get it. I did not have to have the money to pay for it. They would put it on George's bill and George would be there to work for it or do whatever was necessary when they called me to pay them their money back. I could go to any of the stores during the hard times and ask for groceries, like sugar or something, they knew I would work and pay for it. If I had to come over there and plow all day, dig a ditch, if I had to cut some wood or whatever, I would do it. That is the way we survived. We came up through hard times.

They knew anytime they wanted something done they would call for George to come. I always have been an excellent worker. Nobody has ever complained about my work. They would ask me to come over and cut wood and do whatever there was around their house to be done and they always would have something to give me. If it wasn't money, it was something that I could use at the house that would help to make life better for me, and make it better around home for my parents, by helping to lighten their load. With a big family there was always something needed and I always was able to bring it home.

As I developed, I developed in different things, but farming was always part of my life. I had my own chickens, my own pigs, my own animals, when I was a child coming up early in my teens. My mother had hers growing out there in the yard but I got me a place and got me some going too. I would sell some of them sometimes. But most of the time the family ate them. It was the idea of helping my family survive. We did farming and raised different things.

I even had a business of finding nuts in the woods and I would take them up town to sell and make money because we had to have some way of surviving, I would go out in the woods and find hickory nut trees, scaly bark trees, chestnuts and all of that to find something that I could get together to take home to eat or to sell. I used to go out in the woods and I would be gone from home all day long picking nuts one by one. I would look at each nut individually and pick only the good ones. I had a bag picking up chestnuts and what have you, to get together to take back home. When I got them home, I would again examine the nuts one by one, pick out the good ones and get them ready to take them to some of the stores uptown and sell them.

I went uptown and took the nuts I had with me and was selling them for 10 cents a bag with 100 nuts in the bag. That's what I would get for a bag of 100 nuts. I remember there was a white gentleman that I met and he heard that I had nuts to sell and asked me about them.

"Boy what is that you got?"

"I have bags of nuts."

"I want some of your nuts in that bag. How much are you selling them for?"

"10 cents for a bag of 100."

"Alright I will take a bag. If I find one worm in it, I'm going to catch you and I'm going to stretch your neck."

I never did tell my daddy or brought any fear or nothing like that on my mother or dad that somebody was going to stretch my neck. I knew what stretch your neck meant. It meant he was going to hang me. But I just kept it to myself and worked through it. I had gone through the nuts one by one and did my best at whatever I did so I knew there was no worm in the bag. I just went and kept selling nuts. Every time I would get the chance I would go

somewhere else to the other side of town, somebody would buy a bag. All of this money was going back to the house for mama and daddy for their own distributions for the family. The greatest needs that we had were fulfilled.

The only way that I saw how to help my daddy give our family the life that he wanted for us was for me to be a businessman. I didn't even know what a businessman was but I knew I could do more if I was the boss. Nobody was going to tell me what to do. I had to work for those white folks and all of that. Regardless to how strange it was, I was going to do what it took, but it was not going to be forever.

Being a man is not proven by age.

Being a man is proven in actions.

I was a man of integrity at that young age.

I was a man of my word.

I was dependable.

I was willing to work.

I always did my best.

I was responsible and committed to my family.

I knew how to be a provider from a little boy as God was teaching me to be a man.

People expected the best from George Boone even as a child and God was teaching me way back then to be an excellent representative of Him.

When I was 12 years old, my mother and father were ill at the same time. My family's burdens were lightened because I was at least 50% of the family support for that year in my home, through having favor with the white man. I knew there was prejudice around me but some of the things even in a prejudiced life I didn't have to go through. I never was beat on. I never was kicked. I never was hated on by them. I always was just there to do what I was supposed to do and all of that in obedience. But I heard them cursing, slandering, kicking, knocking and beating on black folks and all of that kind of stuff. I bypassed that. I guess I was one of those that they called good Negroes and that was one of the things that happened in my life coming up. I won't say they respected me, I guess God covered me. It wasn't until much later, as an adult, that a serious racial incident happened to me personally.

Later on as I began to grow up I began to get creative in my mind and began to dream of better days and better times for my family. During the time of The Depression eventually everything began to open up. President Franklin D. Roosevelt came in and began to create job systems. I remember when he created the CCC - Civilian Conservation Corps, PWA - Public Work Administration, WPA - Works Progress Administration, TVA - Tennessee Valley of Authority, CWA - Civil Works Administration and I was able to go through those programs and see something else that I could do.

From there I began to progress in my work. I got a little older and I could get out there and go to sawmills and work on farms. This gentleman named Mr. McDonald hired me to come and do some farm work for him, plowing and planting corn and all of that kind of stuff. He worked right along with me and he was a hard worker and so was I. At lunchtime, (in the south we call it dinner and we call dinner, supper) at 12:00 we would stop and rest. We were supposed to knock off for 30 minutes sometimes an hour but most of the time 30 minutes. We knocked off this particular day and I never will forget it. I had my lunch which was nothing but a biscuit with an egg in it. I ate that and it only took me a few minutes. He went on in the house and ate his lunch and when he saw that I was through eating my lunch, he came outside and gave me my orders.

"George while you are resting go out and cut my wife some stove wood."

So during that resting time I was out cutting up wood. So that meant I did not have no rest. We went back to the

I have always done whatever had to be done to keep food on the table and take care of the family.

the family. I have no doubt farming is what made me what I am today.

A Man of God

A Man of Principles

I have the ability to construct things.

Farming is what made me man enough to be an entrepreneur. I can put things together and find another way. I learned that if this isn't working, get something else.

We didn't have a set shift. We got up on the farm early as soon as we could see. That was when we get out and got to work. As soon as I could see - it is time to start working. As soon as I couldn't see it is time to stop working. The working shift on the farm was can see-to-can't see. I knew nothing about the house. I just learned how to cook since 2010. My Grandson, Todd inspired me to want to learn how to cook and as with everything else, I have given it my best and am doing very well. I am still learning things about life because I still have to learn. I was determined to do whatever it took. If I had to go find it right then. I would find it right then. And right now in 2015 if I have to go find it now, I will find it now.

That is why I don't understand all of these people who talk about the bad economy, layoff, recession, all of that is a play thing. Depression times were Depression times! You don't know nothing about stress until you go through A Depression, especially when The Lord cooperates with The Depression. This is a period of my life that I went through!

I remember back in the day that's at 12 years of age how that one year, a drought came through and the crops just burned up. I saw a time when the leaves in the trees fell off in the spring and summer time just like it was fall it was so dry. And we made it work - Anyway we could! Whatever was needed to supplement what daddy did, I looked around outside the home and found it, rabbits, squirrels, birds. As a child, farming was all I knew but I wanted to be a good one.

A year or two later, when they were building the CC Road, I got creative and remember making a slide taking my Daddy's mule and, going to the watermelon patch, up to the hillside and taking them up to the CC Road and selling them to the men that were working for a nickel or dime. That was part of my contribution to the family.

I do remember this though in building a highway in Oxford, Mississippi in my hometown they brought that Number 6 Highway through there. Me and some of the Murphy Boys didn't have these big bulldozers cutting down the trees and pushing the trees back. We were the bulldozers. We were the ones that took the trees down. We were the ones that stacked the logs up. I remember it was just a bunch of black boys working. The foreman would get out there somewhere and talk to us. He made it a field and began to work. Those were hard times.

I started going to the sawmill and working. All of the money that I would make, pretty much went right to my house to help my mother and my dad. Later on after I turned 17 years old, I bought me a car, the first car I bought was a 1929 A Model Ford. I was a big shot then. Everybody knew old George Boone because I had a car.

When I did that I started working from there and still worked in Arm and Clemens Sawmill in Bruce, Mississippi. Sometimes I would be gone for a week before I came back home, but all of my money came back home with me. I was working night and day hauling logs in the daytime and hauling lumber at night, sleeping about two hours a night for about two weeks. That was all the sleep I would get. When I came home I had a pretty good handful of money, probably I would get $1.50 at night and $1.00 in the day time for all that work but I made it. I would take those nickels and dimes and buy a lot of things. That was good money back then. But nevertheless those were hard times.

Even prior to that, I remember after working, there were times I would have to ride my horse, Dan to work. I would ride him so far and then I would leave him tied up at the fork of the road and then I'd ride him back home. Those were hard times working all day. Sometimes I worked 15 hours a day. I took it then as a challenge and I took the challenge with all courage and

ambition and said we are going to make it and it won't be this way always. It brought us up to where we are today. And I thank God for it.

My parents taught me to work. I knew nothing but work even as a child. On a farm doing work meant working in the field. We planted the crops. We cultivated the crops. We harvested the crops. We had to do that for everything that we had to eat in the garden - corn, tomatoes, cabbage, peas and beans. I learned how to do plowing and anything that was necessary.

Sometimes it was raining so hard you could not plant anything. Sometimes we would plant and it would not rain and there would be a drought and everything would be lost and all of our hard work was for nothing.

It meant working in the woods, cutting down trees, cutting them up for wood. It meant that I was a Go-Finder as a child. If we needed something and we didn't have it, it was my responsibility to go and find it. It is somewhere out there. That was the beginning of making me to know that there is something, somewhere to provide for every situation. You just have to go find it. I have been in that.

Farming and the need to provide for my family even way back then is why I had 2, 3, 4 successful different businesses - Barber Shop, Restaurant, Janitorial Service, Landscaping. I have always done whatever had to be done to keep food on the table and take care of point to never call us by our names. He would just talk to the logs. "Log I want you to move." That was our signal to go back to work without being recognized as George, Sam or John. That is just the way they treated us. But I'm thankful today for what God brought us through. I learned a lot.

But nevertheless we thank God for how He brought us through. But through it all I can see a Great God that we serve and how He brought things about. Even our doctors and sickness, home remedies did more for us than the technology we are dealing with now. Some of those home remedies made everything work out alright. It seemed like it was healing in what they said. If it wasn't nothing but get a leaf off the tree, boil it, drink the juice, make a tea out of it we would get alright. We would do better with that leaf that was free than we would do now paying all of these many dollars we are paying for all of these pills. But nevertheless all of that is in our life.

I came up with that tenacity in my mind that I was going to do those things that were required and I say God has sustained me until this day. I feel like that farming was necessary because of the things that God had in my future. I never had no idea of ever being a top man, Diocesan Bishop, Presiding Bishop, Founder or nothing like that. But I always had a religious spark in my life.

I was around 12 years old and they only had a preacher come through once a month at different places and that was where we went to church. My daddy was Methodist and I went to the Methodist Church. A Preacher come through and they sprinkled me. At that time as I got sprinkled I wanted to be baptized. So I went down in my granddaddy's pasture, stopped up a branch and I just kept building it up and building it up until it got high enough of water so I could be baptized in it. The preacher came through and baptized me in my granddaddy Moses Boone's pasture where the animals were grazing.

Later on I was about 15 years old, I went to Philadelphia Missionary Baptist Church and they had a revival going on there and I got down on my knees and I called myself getting religion. I was baptized over again in the Yellow Bush Creek. At the age of 17, John Piggee was the head Deacon there at Philadelphia Missionary Baptist Church and he took me in and started talking to me about being a Jr. Deacon. Later on he put me in training as a Jr. Deacon and every time he would get ready to pray he wanted me to kneel down with him and I heard him as he kneeled down to pray. He prayed the same prayer every time he got down to pray. "We come again on our sin bended knees. The things you told us what to do we found out not how to do those things but please Sir have mercy." And that's what he taught me. But I thought in my spirit that there was a better way. A better way than that. I'm thankful. I love my Lord.

As I grew up into a young adult, I was still very concerned about my family including my 12 sisters. I won't say I took care of all of them, because really when I was 12 years old, some of them had married and were on their own like Victoria, Arie, Esther. But all of those that my mother had like Frankie, Lucille, Charity, they were older than me and they were included with me in whatever I was doing to help the family survive and take care of things.

As they grew up I was protective of them. They always looked to me. Some of them asked me about some of the guys when they started dating and I gave them advice about men. I tried to help them but some of them I couldn't. We embraced ourselves as children and those years bring even now many great memories to my mind.

From 12 to 18 years of age I was quite known as one of the youngsters who would break any horse, mule or anything to ride. I didn't care how he bucked, what kind of horse he was, whether he was a Tennessee Walker, whether he was a Quarter Horse or any of them. I would get on any of their backs. All they knew is if you get George Boone he will ride him. And I was also that way about wrestling.

The truth of it of my lifetime, even when I was working, especially down in Bruce, Mississippi where we had maybe about 20 or 30 men out there in the sawmill working, they had a way of initiating. I told them if they come one

by one, I would take every single one of them. I was that bad. I cannot remember my back being put on the ground but about twice in my life.

One of them was my cousin, Shepherd Boone, he put my back on the ground. But out of all of those other fellows, my back did not hit the ground. I kept that my main thing, I maintained it. Guys would hear about me and come from out of town and come to put my back on the ground. My back wasn't hitting the ground I would say from 13 years old until 18 or 20. Even when I went in the Army nobody was able to ever grab me that could put my back on the ground. I could keep it off the ground. I've had them pick me up and couldn't put me down. I would throw them in the fall. That's how good I was. And I love it. It is in my genes today. I would stop eating anytime if somebody came out there and said they wanted to wrestle. It's still in my genes. If I see somebody wrestling right today, I almost want to grab them as old as I am right now.

There is one thing that Vassar Lockhart, my brother-in-law used to say. "If I could ever put your back on the ground I would be satisfied." Never could do it.

Sometimes I think many of the things that happened to me in my childhood day, God had a purpose in it to help me to be able to go where we are today - through the many things as I went through hard times and all of that.

CHAPTER 2

ARMY

Buck Private Boone

O.B. Barnes

Mama

December 7, 1941, the Japanese bombed Pearl Harbor, Hawaii. World War II was raging. President Franklin D. Roosevelt decided it was time for the United States to get involved in fighting this war. I was drafted into the United States Army December 7, 1942 in Camp Shelby, Mississippi. I was Honorably Discharged January 6, 1946. I met a friend, O.B. Barnes who was sworn in the same day I was. From that day we were never separated. We traveled together and were discharged together.

Those were probably the longest four years of my mother's life. That hurt my mother so bad because I was her only son and the world was at war. I could have been killed. Back then black people thought a white man could do anything and white people pretty much did whatever they wanted to do. She was crying and sent me to Mr. Ramsey who was known as the white man in town who could fix almost anything for Black folks.

"Go to Mr. Ramsey and tell him to keep you from going to the Army."

I went to see him.

"Mr. Ramsey, I'm supposed to be drafted into the army is there anything you can do so I don't have to go?"

"No, no, just go on in the Army."

That was the end of that. Sometimes White people did what they wanted to do. They had their own laws. From there, later on we were ready to be drafted to go overseas.

Taking my mind back to December 7, 1942, the year after the Japanese attacked Pearl Harbor when I was inducted into the United States Army, being my mother's only son that was a dreadful and strainful time for me and for my mother. I may have expressed to you further in other chapters about being religiously inclined all my life to a degree. I remember after I was sworn in the army, when I got on the train headed to Camp Tyson, Tennessee, I was singing a song, "Walk with me Lord, walk with me, all along this tedious journey I want you to walk with me."

And I think about how that the Lord has carried me all through my army life, the hard things I experienced in my army life, seeing so many thousands of men killed and brought to destruction by the great machine guns and bombs and what have you. I say but the Lord spared my life and that makes me very thankful today. I thank Him for it today.

But thinking about my mother and how torturing it was for her for those years, that she couldn't hear from me for sometimes two months, she couldn't hear nothing, didn't know whether I was living or not. No mail or nothing was in existence. And my sister, Mae would tell me how she would worry and how she would cry. She stayed with her all the time and said Mama would just cry and she was singing a song, "Bring my son back home." All of those things were very torturous. But even in that I learned how to trust God and learned to know Him better and love Him more.

Mae

After being drafted into the armed forces, I moved up to Breckenridge Kentucky. There was another church there called the Tried Stone Baptist Church. I said I believe I can make it here and I went and joined that church.

We went to New Orleans, Louisiana and I met a Church of God in Christ preacher by the name of Elder Utah Smith. I wasn't saved. I was just doing the best I could. But anyway I went there. I went that night and the preacher was preaching, a sister got happy, run up and hugged me and Elder Utah Smith spoke to me.

"Soldier don't get nothing in your mind. That's a holy hug. Ain't nothing to it, just a holy hug." He preached and pricked my heart about being saved and being filled with the Holy Ghost.

But O.B. Barnes was the one that witnessed to me and let me know I needed the Holy Ghost! He started witnessing to me in Tennessee and he carried it all the way to the Jungles of New Guinea. We were inducted into the army and discharged the same day. We were never separated. The Lord put us together. Everywhere we moved to, our bunks were right together. I had never heard of the Holy Ghost. But I was a Jr. Deacon in the Baptist Church and thought that was good enough.

Every once in a while my foot would slip. We would go to the store shopping and get something that we were going to carry back to the barracks and we would sit down and eat. I would see some good looking women coming out of the store and I would drop off and detour. When I walked back in the barracks, Brother O.B. Barnes was waiting for me. "George I told you, you need the Holy Ghost." He stayed on me. He was always talking to me about getting the Holy Ghost, getting the Holy Ghost, getting saved and being saved. He made me feel like I could not live right without the Holy Ghost. So that is why I sought for the Holy Ghost.

ARMY DAYS OTHER EVENTS

I went to Basic Training in Camp Tyson, Tennessee, Breckenridge, Kentucky and New Orleans, Louisiana.

In New Orleans, Louisiana, when I was inducted into the Army something happened to my hand and my hand was all swollen up. I went to a young man and he was a Corporal at the time, I told him I wanted to be dismissed from KP Duty which was Kitchen Police duty. I was washing dishes and all of that. He was harsh, called me a name and told me to get in the kitchen and go to work. I took my swollen hand and went on back in. Even after that occurred and they sent us overseas I never did serve under that Corporal anymore. I had somebody else.

Then I went to Pearl Harbor, Hawaii and then to The Jungles of New Guinea. Traveling from Hawaii to The Jungles of New Guinea, I spent 43 days on the water with no sight of land. While sailing, I had an experience that I will never forget. One of the men aboard the ship sailing the Pacific Ocean made a mistake and fell off the ship. In that vast amount of water, the Captain sent a small raft and some men out to rescue him; it was a great battle to save this one man's life and as I relate this experience, one can understand how cruel the waters can be; at times they could see this man as he bobbed up and down in those mean waters; at times, he was completely out of sight and then someone on board would give that desperate cry "There he is!" When the men in the rescue raft finally caught him, they had quite a fight rescuing him as he was fighting to save his life and losing it all the time, but they got him, hurt and bleeding, put him in the rescue boat and brought him back to the Seascamp.

I stayed there in the Jungles of New Guinea four or five months, left there and went to San Fernando, Millender Bay in the Philippine Islands. Finally we went into Tokyo, Japan where I was discharged from.

I had several jobs in the army. I started as Buck Private, charding calvary horses, then they were disbanded and I went into Quarter Master Service, getting food up to the guys on the front line. I was then elevated to technician of files, I had 17 or 18 men under me with the assignment to go forward and build warehouses to store food and other supplies. I also did Guard Duty on this or that particular warehouse, wherever I was assigned. When all of the warehouses were built, Captain Balding said. "I am going to keep your rank Technician 5 and make you the company barber." I had been studying to be a barber under O. B. Barnes and I kept on practicing until I got to be very good. I never thought about the Army as a career.

I wanted to get back home and do my thing.

I wanted to have something of my own.

That was basic to me.

Create your own.

Always want to do and have something I can handle myself.

I didn't want to be told do this, do that.

I always felt like it won't be like this always.

ARMY THE JUNGLES OF NEW GUINEA

When I say Jungle it was a Jungle!

We came in on a ship, got on barges and had the barge go as far as it could and we worked our way into the jungle. You just leave the water and walk into a bunch of thick weeds and woods. You take machetes and cut your way back in. They didn't have machines. Just like in my youth in Mississippi for Highway 6, we were the machines. We had to manhandle ourselves cutting through all of that by crawling, walking, carrying our back packs, picks and shovels. We had to dig foxholes and all of that. It was no problem for me but it was a problem for some of them because some of them knew nothing about hard work outside in the heat. I was able to maintain because I was used to hard work.

We came across snakes and all kind of crazy animals. I was never attacked by anything but they were there. Something about the jungle made you hysterical if you didn't have yourself together in your head. I've seen men just work their way through the thick weeds and trees, take off running in the jungle, leave us and we don't see them no more. There are spirits out there in that jungle. There are things that happen and you don't know where it comes from. I saw grown men soldiers standing up with their guns and crying. I've seen something come up and disturb us so much that men would jump out of the barracks and start hollering and screaming, and it looks like you see something running this way and running that way. At the time I felt sorry for them.

I never had those problems or went into nothing myself. I always figured it was a better way than this. I was able to maintain my right mind because of growing up in hard times. I was in better shape for it because some of those city boys couldn't take it. I always kept perseverance in my spirit.

Even before I got saved it was the Lord who kept His hands on me and kept my mind intact.

It was so hot in the jungle that I saw the heat just blister the skin on the natives' backs. The skin would just pucker up, bust open then hang down. It was just pitiful. You could smell them, they smelled like wild animals. And when the natives would come through the jungle, the king would have a staff in one hand and a machete in the other and everybody else followed him. He would be cool and comfortable with no heavy load. The women carried the baby, water, bags of grain and were just happy to be there.

The conditions were unbearable. You couldn't drink the water and you just did without water until some fresh water got dropped off the next day. Taking baths and all of that had to wait and you just endured until you get some rescue.

Elder George Flemings of the Church of God In Christ baptized me later on in the Bay of New Guinea in the Name of the Father, Son and Holy Ghost. I wrote back home and told my mother and my sisters and all about it. I didn't know of any Boone with the Holy Ghost. I was

I was baptized in the Bay of New Guinea

the first Boone that I heard tell of getting the Holy Ghost. But I began to write back and tell them that I had the Holy Ghost and it was a burden on me in my heart for them to get saved too. I wasn't a Bible reader but I do know somewhere in the Song of Solomon it says, *It was but a little that I passed from them, but I found him whom my soul loveth. I held him, and would not let him go, until I had brought him into my mother's house, and into the chamber of her that conceived me. Song of Solomon 3:4*

My soul began to burn saying that I had to witness to my family about the Holy Ghost.

On the 4th Sunday in May, May 28, 1944, me and some of the soldiers set up a small tent in the mud and jungle rot and began to have service. One of my distant cousins, Brother Nimrod Boles was in the Army too and the Lord called him to preach. He preached his first sermon there in the Jungles of New Guinea and I was his first convert. His sermon was what Jesus said, *I must work the works of him that sent me, while it is day: the night cometh, when no man can work. St. John 9:4.* That message did something. It made me feel like I wanted whatever it was, if it was the Holy Ghost or whatever it was that would make me get closer to the Lord I wanted it. It just drew me closer to the Lord. The mud was so contaminated from the dead bodies, they said you would get jungle rot if you got it on your hands. I got down on my hands and knees at an old orange crate in the mud

and water in the Jungles of New Guinea and I received the gift of the Holy Ghost speaking in tongues. God's anointing was surely on me. The mud never affected my hands. Brother O.B. Barnes was playing the guitar while I was receiving the Holy Ghost, it sound like that Guitar was saying, JESUS.

TOE JOE

Toe Joe was Brother O.B Barnes' dog and he was a pet to the soldiers there in that particular camp. Everybody knew, everybody respected old Toe Joe just like he was somebody.

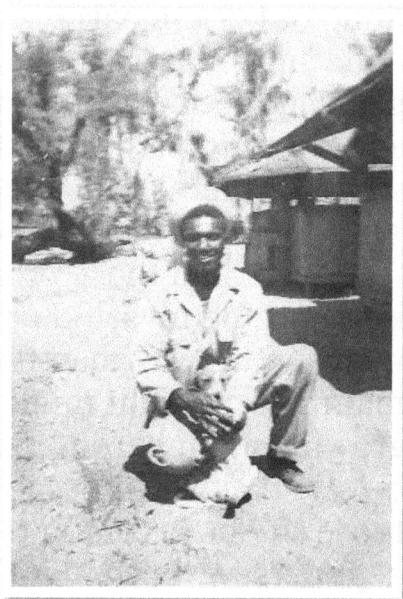

I am holding Toe Joe

He was everybody's dog. He was a mixed dog, a spotted dog. We got him over there and he was just one that O.B. found out there struggling around out there in the Jungles of New Guinea. I know he didn't bring him back to the states. We were discharged and we left him over there but he was a pet and company for us all.

DAVE TERRY

Dave Terry was one of my comrades in the army. He was the one that helped me in his way of what he called torturing me. He didn't like me and I didn't like him at the beginning. I don't know why he really didn't like me. But he knew I wasn't afraid of

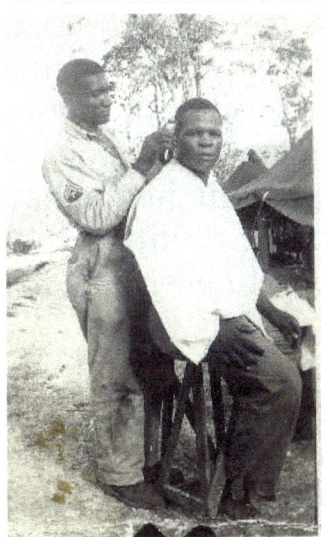

I am cutting Dave Terry's hair

him and he was a bully in the camp. And he felt me, I said, "Now when you come this way it's going to be on." He always felt that but he never did bring it. But when it all was said and done, being the bully in the camp, I saw him once slap a young man and kill him. Slapped him! They were gambling in the dice game and Dave Terry just jumped up and slapped that young man. He fell about 10 feet from the dice game and that man went stumbling backwards. They put him in the hospital and he died.

I wasn't saved during that game and that is where my hate really came from. I said, "If he ever crosses me I'm going to hurt him." He knew that. And of course he just kept it against me. Kept it against me.

After I got the Holy Ghost, Elder George Flemings, Brother O.B. Barnes and I were standing up talking when Dave came up and interfered with the conversation. He was challenging me and I said nothing to him. He came up to me, slapped me, spit in my face, took his knife out and swung it across my face two or three times. I never did anything to him. It was something about the Holy Ghost I

Elder George Flemings, Brother O.B. Barnes & Myself

just couldn't hate him anymore. I couldn't get back at him although before I got saved, I had purposed to kill him.

That born again experience is something else.

When you are born again, you are a new creature.

AND GOD KNOWS THAT WAS IT!

The Holy Ghost turned my hatred for Dave Terry into love.

Nevertheless in about 10 minutes, somebody stabbed him and put him in the hospital and he stayed in there for about a month. He came out and talked to me. Man to man. "Boone, Look. Let me tell you. Most of my folks is sanctified and the reason why I did you like that is that I heard you got the Holy Ghost and I wanted to see if you really was saved."

Me and that fellow got to be the best of friends. If I could take $2,000.00 and fly him in here where you all could see him, I'd do it in a minute. I don't know where he is. I guess he is dead now. I lost track of him. Yes sir. I would have had him to come to my church at any cost even if they had to wheelchair him in there. But that's it. That is how close we were.

After that, anybody - guys drinking and just rough guys say anything, like want to throw something at me or call me out of my name or something like that, Dave Terry would say with authority in his voice, "Hey that's mine, I'll take that one. Say it again." He was so tough they all called him the Bull in the Woods! That is how tough Dave was. Great big double jointed guy, I loved that guy.

We got separated before we came back to the states. I don't know what happened. They began to send me here and him there. I even called Houston, Texas to see if there were any Terry's that I could get in touch with and I never could run him down any more.

PHILIPPINES

The Japanese were looking at the Philippine women and the soldiers took advantage of them and I felt sorry for them. Those poor women would do anything just to have a piece of bread. In the Philippines the weather varied but it never got too hot or too cold.

I have been to the Jungles of New Guinea, The Philippines and Japan. In all of those places I walked into total devastation and in all of those places I had to fix and make ready for myself and others. I just saw what had to be done and I did it. I am convinced that was part of God's training for where He has me now.

And of course during that time, I did complete my entrance toward salvation. I did get to really know the Lord for who He is. I knew Him in the way of protection, I knew Him in the way of being my great battle axe, my protector, my friend. He showed Himself to me in many ways. And of course I met some hardship.

There was a gun that the Japanese had hidden over behind the mountain. And you could hear that gun go off and then after so many seconds, you could hear the explosion coming our way and it had bullets in it. When it would hit the ground after so many seconds, the ground shook under us and it began to

Technician 5 Boone

explode with unbelievable noise, then when it would explode something from that would explode and it would just take care of the whole area reaching a great portion of the area that was a long way from where they shot the gun. Many of our people got killed and we were on the beachhead. We would take our shovels and dig down to have a hole to hide in, but that gun was so powerful it would shake the ground, so when we know anything we would be back up on top of the ground almost. We would take our spade, dig a hole and get back down in the hole.

I remember this, I woke up one morning in the foxhole and my First Sergeant was sitting up in front of me and I got up where I could kind of peep out and I could just see the coconut trees all laying down and things was just real quiet and you couldn't hear nothing. I began to look in front of me. And there was my First Sergeant sitting there and it looked like he had a stick or something holding his head up. But that is where some of the explosion from that gun went over me and got him in the back of the head and blood had run down from his wound and congealed from his lap to his nose and was holding his head up and that was him sitting there dead. And I had been favored by God. I was still alive.

I got up along with others and we left that area and as we came back to the area to get reunited back with whoever was living, we saw those white crosses where the Red Cross had come in and buried those bodies. You could just see acres of white crosses. Everywhere you saw a white cross it was a dead body.

I was on the beachheads, San Sabron and San Franneda in the Philippines, getting food to the soldiers on the front lines. There was no mercy shown by the enemy. The men were being killed so fast, they would just stack up the bodies like cordwood, over 5 feet high, until the next few hours or days when the Red Cross would come by, pick up the bodies, then bury them. That horrific sight of death, with me overshadowed by God's infinite mercy, has never left me.

From that standpoint, many things came to my heart that are helping me today just to know how determined God was to accomplish His purpose in my life by bringing me back from the Army. Safe. In my right mind. Ready to serve Him. We do know about so many more things now.

JAPAN

After the United States dropped the bomb, Japan was different. It was just torn up. The people were pitiful. Bodies were floating in the water everywhere, people were homeless with nothing to eat. We were not supposed to help them but we let a little boy so malnourished he was

And I had been favored by God. I was still alive.

starving to death stay with us. He appeared to be no older than 8 or 9 years old. When he began to get his strength back we discovered he was really an 18 year old young man. When I was on my way out, the soldiers were discussing how he deceived them. I don't know if they put him out of the barracks or killed him when they found out how old he was or not.

Some of the Japanese people were beginning to get back to where they were moving around a little bit and were in the process of cleaning up and I didn't have to stay there for very long. People were cleaning up but the smell was unbearable. In Japan there was snow and ice and all kinds of weather.

After Japan then back to the states, landing in California, sent back to where I started to Camp Shelby, Mississippi on January 6, 1946 I was honorably discharged from the United States Army.

GETTING BAPTIZED IN JESUS' NAME

Back there farming was all I knew, but I wanted to be a good one. I started building myself up around farm life. Even when I came out of the Army, I went into Agricultural School. I wanted to learn how to grow everything and know everything about it. I bought my first farm in 1946 from my Uncle L. Boone. I bought all of my own farm equipment, with the farm and started on that. My mules I bought when I came out of the Army were named Fred and George. When I came out of the Army I really was just intending to settle down on the farm, raise livestock and grow stuff.

I didn't get baptized in Jesus' Name until I was discharged and got back home by District Elder Rush L. Lockhart, Sr. shortly after he baptized me, he became my father-in-law.

CHAPTER 3

MY WIFE, MAE DEE BOONE AND OUR YOUNG FAMILY

When I met my wife, she was in her teen age years, must have been 16 or 17 years old. The reason why I met her, it was other guys and they had devilment in their eyes and her daddy was so protective. The other guys said, "You ain't never going to get to see Lockhart's daughter." I said, "Who ain't going to see Lockhart's daughter? Who me? Who is it that is so bad that I can't go and see if I want to see her?" I went there and her father wasn't home. Her mother wasn't home. Just she and her brothers were there. I never went up on the porch.

Elder Lockhart

I had started working in the sawmill making a little more than $1.00 a day. I bought me a car by that time a 1929 A Model Ford. She was standing there looking out the door. I was walking back and forth around the house trying to get a good look at her. Finally when I saw her I said, "If I write you will you answer my letters?" We had never met. She didn't say anything.

After I got the Holy Ghost, I wrote Elder Lockhart because he was the only Holy Ghost preacher in my hometown of Oxford, Mississippi, that I felt, was living right. I asked him, "Tell your daughter to send me some scriptures. I'm saved. I have the Holy Ghost and I want to know all I can about the Bible." So he told her and she sent me some scriptures and I used to read them. In one of her letters, she said, "You remember you asked if you wrote me would I return your letters? I guess this is it. I guess I am returning your letters."

I had a group of cousins wild as a deer, just women chasers and they always tried to get me involved in that. I stayed away from that to that degree. The only children I have my wife had them for me. Thanks be to God, when I married her, I married a virgin.

I went down and I met her in Alcorn College. Another friend was going to see the girl he did marry who was in school there. I told him, "I'll go down there with you." Mae Dee was in and she came and met me. She was prompt, looking good, that didn't move me so much because there were other girls that were nice looking too. But something about her just kind of stuck on me and we started talking. Finally I made a statement to her some way that she saw I was somewhat interested. Maybe we could start talking as boyfriend and girlfriend. The door was open and I didn't have no problem there and then we just kept on talking. She talked about preachers a little bit. She asked me, "You aren't a preacher are you? I don't want no preacher. I have enough preachers in my family." I just talked all around that question.

She wanted to go to her Daddy's and Mama's house for Easter and she didn't

Elder & Mother Lockhart

have the money for the trip. Well I had plenty money sticking all out of my pocket just to show off because I was young. But I did have money because I

Mae Dee

was a hard working man. I said, "What would your daddy think if I gave you the money to come home?" She said, "I think it would be alright." I said, "Well find out and I will send you the money."

She was in Alcorn College and wanted to be a Dietician because of all of the money she was going to make. I told her, "Don't worry about that, when you get me you got money."

She came home and we met then and we started talking. When I really met my wife and sat down and talked with her, from that time I guess in about two more months me and Mae Dee were married.

Two weeks before that I was supposed to have been marrying another girl in Mackenzie, Tennessee. I just went to Alcorn College to visit Mae Dee and me and this other girl were engaged. It wasn't nothing wrong with her as far as I was concerned. It wasn't nothing wrong with me. But God just cut it like that. Her name was Evelyn Howard.

When I saw that I wasn't going to marry Evelyn, I told my sister, Easter to write Evelyn. That is where I chickened out and I knew it was going to hurt the girl so bad and I didn't know how I was going to do it. I said just write her a letter and tell her I changed my mind about getting married. And I thought she did but she didn't. There wasn't no wedding like you all have now. I just needed the preacher and her and that would have been it. I was just going to go get married. I had no more contact with her. And I didn't find out until years later that Easter did not write to her.

I didn't like the name Mae Dee so I started calling her Mary. I changed her last name so I said she might as well come all the way on over with me and let me change the first name too. Change it to a name that I like.

I asked her father about marrying her and he said yes at first. Then he went to trying to back out after different ones was talking to him. Mae Dee's cousin, Sam Williams said to her father, "If you let that girl marry George he is going to kill her."

But I got her a ring, her father saw the ring and the children and all of them let him know we were going to her uncle's house to get married. Her father found out I was serious and we were getting married. My wife's Uncle Talmon, was the one who took me to her house to pick her up, and took us to his house in Oxford, Mississippi on August 25, 1946 a Sunday Afternoon and the preacher was there.

After we were married about six or seven years Elder Lockhart broke down laughing and said, "George at first I didn't want you to marry my daughter, Mae Dee but now I'm glad you did." I'm driving all those new cars down there, she was just superb hadn't heard about nothing that I did to hurt her, and everything was good for her. We were living together as husband and wife, I was a minister and God blessed us to be serving Him in the beauty of holiness. I NEVER laid a hand on my wife to hurt her.

She never told me why she married me. I think she thought I was a good provider like her father. But I'll tell you, a woman working back in my day when I married her, like you all now, the wife working? No! We brought it all in and they took care of the house and the family. I heard my father say, when I was at an early age, a woman can throw more out of the window with a teaspoon than a man can bring in the front door with a shovel. But Mary knew how to handle money and the house. We never lost one dollar.

So I don't bother with why she said yes. I just set out to be the best man I knew how to be. I learned how to be a man, husband and father when I was a little boy. You married. You took care of that family. If you had 12 children they were going to eat like you had one. All were going to live well.

My wife benefited today from the things that I purposed in my heart for that little girl Alberta Hill. One of the things I can say strictly to the glory of God, since I married her, she has never seen me when I couldn't put my hand on a dollar.

That is one thing I challenge the young men of today with, running around with not a dime in their pocket. I don't see how they can do it. Since I've been a man and started making money I always had money. I've never been broke. I always kept a dollar. That is one of the things that help me to try to mold young men and impress upon them that they are not to be the tail but be the head. And for that cause I appreciate the hard times.

After we got married and I was about 26 years old, a man was operating a barber shop and he got killed. I was a barber and my wife's Uncle Leslie told me there was a chance for me to own a barber shop. It wasn't a lot of barber shops then in Oxford, so I left the farm. We opened up a barber shop and restaurant, cooking hamburgers and dinners. They called it the Boone Barber Shop. I had a public shower put in the place. The shower was for different guys working and coming out from the sawmill. On their way home they would stop by the barber shop take a shower that they paid for, buy their dinner and continue on their way.

I operated the barber shop, and the restaurant was run by my wife, my sister, Easter and also I had some other girls there. I dwelled on that until I decided to come to Detroit. I was going to stay in Mississippi but something happened.

I saw, then experienced racism. Firsthand. You saw the sign that said white and even if the other place didn't say colored you know that is where you go. If it was a restaurant they would have the window and Negroes went to that window and had to stand outside to get their food.

But I got tired of the way they were doing black men especially black soldiers. They went and served in the Army and when they went into public places I saw how white people would talk to them. I'm listening at that and just thought there has to be something better than that. I just thought I would come up north and maybe it would be better but I still wasn't in a hurry to leave Mississippi.

I knew people personally who were lynched, beaten, burned, killed, destroyed.

I knew people personally who were lynched, beaten, burned, killed, destroyed. My wife's relatives, the Ivy's were pretty well known. They had a little money, nice property. The white people burned, hung, killed, broke in and beat on some of them. They did all that kind of stuff. My daddy went and asked for the ashes from one of the boys that they took and burned, so his family could bury him. I lived through all of that.

It affected me to this extent. I knew this was happening and I knew it would happen to me if I got caught in the wrong place. I didn't want to bring my children up in this environment. I did not want my family exposed to that.

But I knew how they felt about us. I stayed in a boundary there. I never got out of order. I didn't want to be around their little old girls. I didn't want to be white. Other than taking care of business or working, I was not around them that much. I never had none of them to come up and curse me out or beat me or kick me and call me some kind of old nigger. And I never had no problem working with nobody.

But that was not enough for the prejudiced white people. You did not want to be caught out at night in Mississippi and one night I was. One incident where racism came directly to me and my family made me leave and move to Detroit.

MISSISSIPPI, RACISM - TIME TO LEAVE

I was looking for a church and went up to a place called Coldwater, Mississippi. On the way driving back, with my wife, her cousin Robert Thacker and our newborn son Ralph in the car, it happened. Even though I was not speeding the police pulled me over. They made us get out of the car, searched my wife and the baby's bag, threw all of our stuff on the ground, like they were throwing away whiskey or something. They made me stand outside the car and when they finished going through the car, he told me to get back in the car. I got ready to get back in the car I saw the police standing behind me, pulling up his Billy club and I heard a voice in my head say, "he is getting ready to hit you." By the time I turned around he hit me on the left back of my head and I felt real dizzy and was dazed. As I was driving I rubbed my hand over the back of my head and saw blood on my hand. I went to Dr. Little that next morning and he said, I did get a fracture there. For over a year there were certain ways I would turn my head and I would get real dizzy. That was when I said this is enough. I was there for another five months then took my wife and son and we moved to Detroit, Michigan in November 1947.

I didn't even go back to sell the farm I bought. I kept the farm for a few years somebody came by and wanted it and I let them have it.

DETROIT, MICHIGAN

My sister, Myrtle was here first and she told me about everything being what it was. If I hadn't been an entrepreneur I never would have made it. I had my barber tools and came in making more money than I was making before I started my job at Plymouth Motor Car. That is the truth. In January 1948, I was hired by the Plymouth Motor Car Company and worked there for twelve years.

All of the glory and praise goes to God for Him bringing to life my dream as a child. I settled in my mind that with God's help I was going to be the best provider I could be in taking care of my family. When we got married, I opened a bank account for my wife in Oxford, Mississippi, and her bank account was open and waiting for her when she got to Detroit. "I don't want you, if you want to do something for yourself or for your mother, to have to come and ask me for some money. I want you to just be able to do whatever you want to do because we are working together to maintain our family."

I would watch the account to see how much money was there and when it got to a certain point, I would add some more money in it. I never asked her what she did with it because we were and still are a team. We work together to maintain our home and family. She worked just as hard inside the house as I did outside. That is how it was. From the beginning, it has always been that way.

Right today if they said I was an abusive man it wouldn't bother me because I know better. Job said, my record is on high. That doesn't bother me. I know. God knows. My wife knows.

She had confidence in my word as her husband. Always. Not a child that has ever been born in my house ever saw me when I couldn't provide the best for them. I've been that way ever since and they just took my word for that. My wife never asked whether or not we could afford something. If there was something she wanted to do, I had already provided the money and the means. I trusted her completely because she was handling the money and the bills inside the house. Her hands were free to work within the boundaries of whatever she thought was best for our home and family. And she always did an excellent job.

There has never been a time a man called on the phone or knocked on the door about an unpaid bill. Nobody ever threatened to take our cars, house or cut off the lights, gas or the water. God always provided a way for me to take care of my family because that is what a man is supposed to do.

> *She worked just as hard inside the house as I did outside.*

FAMILY

All of my boys in coming up, every one of them, I made sure they had their own bank account. My little girls, when they were five years old, I took out an insurance policy. A man came to the house and said it was the wrong kind of policy and I should cash it in. When I cashed them in, I put it in their names and at five years old I started every one of my children with a bank account. I made sure that happened. It was important for me to open bank accounts for my children in the 50's and 60's when some blacks did not do that. It was something that I came through hard times and remembered how independent it makes you feel if you could have a dollar you could put your hands on that was yours. I was not going to see my children broke. All of this came at the expense of working three jobs, going to school and running a business.

I have managed to work, I managed to toil, I managed to do everything to provide for my family as God blessed me with a strong mind, health and strength.

My Family

When I moved to Detroit, I first lived with John and Myrtle Fears, my sister and brother-in-law. But when I brought Mary and Ralph up here I had found a place with Bill Gaines. His wife had left him so we took the rest of the flat and we lived together there for a while. Then my Pastor, Elder Leaston had a place on Vine on the west side and we got that apartment.

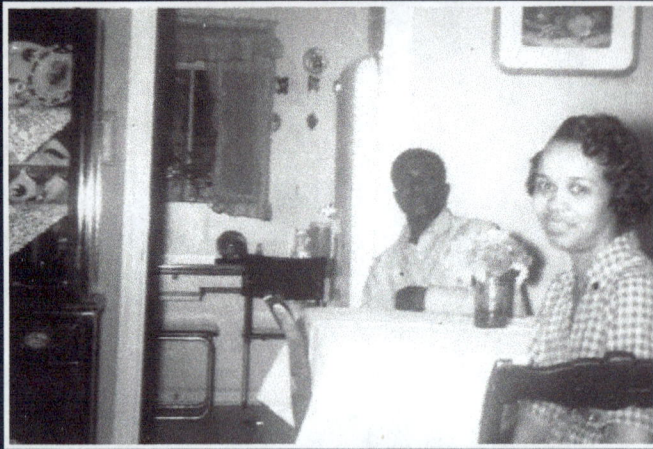
Mary & Myself

I am holding Lil Ralph

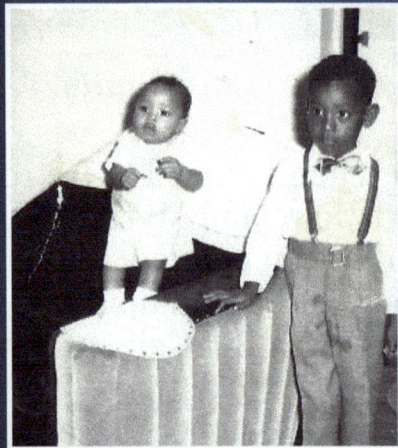
Lil Ralph & Lil GeRonald

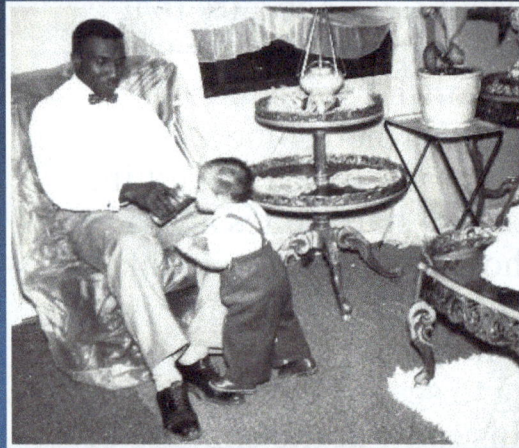
Lil GeRonald & Myself

Lil Charles, I am holding Baby
Alfred in 1956

Ralph, GeRonald, Charles,
Alfred, I am holding Lil
Sharon in 1958

*I knew how to be a provider from a little boy as
God was teaching me to be a man.*

My Family in 1960

Mary & Myself

Baby Sharon blessed in 1956

Alfred & Charles

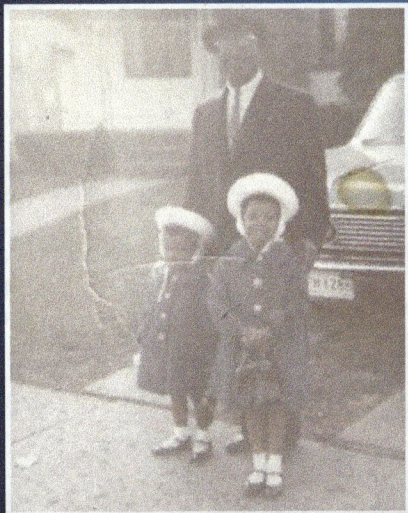
Lil Sharon, Lil Shirley &
Myself

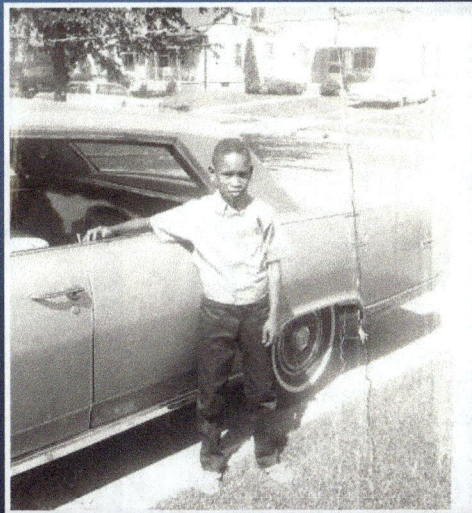
Alfred

*have managed to work, I managed to toil, I managed to do everything
to provide for my family as God blessed me with a strong mind,
health and strength.*

Myself

My Family

GeRonald, Charles & Alfred

My Family

Sharon & Shirley

Mary, Sharon & Shirley

All of the glory and praise goes to God for Him bringing to life my dream as a child. I settled in my mind that with God's help I was going to be the best provider I could be in taking care of my family.

CHAPTER 4

BARBER SHOP - MR. HAROLD ELLIS

I always was aggressive when it comes down to having something from a child up.

That was the time I decided the Lord was going to bless me. I worked three jobs, with this schedule:

I would get up at 5:00 a.m.

Go to the Plymouth Motor Car Company until 3:00 p.m.

Come back to Harold Ellis' Barbershop, stay there from 3:00 p.m. - 6:00 p.m.

Leave there and go downtown to school at 6:30 p.m. - 7:30 p.m.

Get out of school and be at church at 8:00 p.m.

After church I would do janitorial work at Dr. Boyd, the Dentist's office, on 8 Mile Road.

Working in the Barber Shop

Mr. Ellis's Barber Shop

Mr. Ellis was the apprentice barber
even though he was the proprietor.
But he wanted to know how to cut hair.
I was the barber with a Master Barber's
License meaning I was a full-fledged
licensed barber, who could bring others
under me. The barbers were James
Scott, Harold Ellis, Louis Girty and I.

It wasn't so much like it was today,
today you get an appointment. Back
then you just come as you were and
sometimes you would be overcharged,
sometimes get a discussion going, and
say I got here first, no I got here first
and there could be an argument.

I worked so hard my eyes began to
get bad and the eye Doctor said my
resistance was down so low he
couldn't give me an eye test. I would
get up and go to the bathroom and
sometimes I would fall out in there
from working three jobs.

CHAPTER 5

MENDOTA - ALFRED'S DEATH - BELLEVILLE

I came here by myself and stayed for two months. I sold my car then went back and got Ralph and Mary.

In the latter part of 1948, as soon as they started building around Detroit they opened up a place on Mendota and 8 Mile Road. I went there and put in an order for a brand new house to build for my family. It was a 30 year mortgage but we paid it off in seven years. I didn't want a mortgage. We worked to do that. Mary cooperated with me.

Mendota Home

I looked at the land when I went there and it was barren. I had to get flowers in the yard, and some chickens, that was from my days on the farm, loving livestock. Couldn't have no other animals but chickens were enough. To this day I still have to have living things growing around me. I had to have a garden with everything I could

In our garden

grow. Greens, tomatoes everything and I had to have some beauty too, so I planted flowers which I love. It was my brand new home. All of the neighbors respected us. Nobody trying to cast us down and push us or nothing like that. I had no problem with my neighbors.

I started working at Plymouth Motor Car Company on Mt. Elliott in Detroit. The day shift foreman came up to put me on afternoons, and I knew God's calling was upon my life and I couldn't work afternoons and I wanted to be at church at night. I began to think and pray about it and they lightened up and God blessed me to be able to stay on day shift. The next time they came to talk to me about it, I had no option because they had made the decision that I would go on afternoons. It was a done deal. And I decided to start a landscaping business.

If you want anything you've got to work for it and save your money. I taught my children how to save money, not just spend all they made. I taught them how to budget it to have money in your pocket, be able to take care of your future and the things that you are engaged in. I kept my boys right up under me. Mary was the bookkeeper and she kept excellent records.

I got out there and bought a 1953 Chevrolet and got a trailer. I got a push lawn mower, rakes, shovel and a hoe and said, "I'm going to go out here and make me some money."

While I was working in Oak Park, Michigan, a lady called me over. "Come on and let me talk to you, sit down. I know about gardening. I'm going to help you. I know all these folks out here. If you want to get started I will tell them about you." And she told them.

The next day I had a job and I did such a good job, anytime somebody stopped me to do something, I would jump off the truck and do that. The next day another job opened up then I did some more. The next day 3, 4, 5, 6, 7, jobs came from that job. Then I went and bought me a pick-up truck, got that filled up with equipment. After that I bought another truck and built my business up. When I got through working there I had 150 jobs a week.

I brought all of my boys in when they were very young.

Ralph was 12.

GeRonald was 8.

Charles was 6.

Alfred was 5.

My boys would be there on that job with me. All of my boys are taught by my words and my example to do excellent work. When you look at my bushes right now and they are trimmed and done right that is my son, Charles. All of them are good at that. Not one of them ever went on a paper route. I worked them right there by my side. I kept them like that right up under me.

They left from the landscaping business to their own businesses or whatever they wanted to go in. I kept them out of the street. They went to school, then came on back and went to landscaping. Every week that they worked they got money to put in the bank, I did not let them spend it. After the employees got paid, I paid my boys, they put their money in the bank and we carried the business like that.

I wanted my sons to be honest. I taught them if they are going to work, come on and do a good job, be faithful. Don't try to cut corners. Some of those outsiders that I brought in they were goldbricks. Every time they get a chance they were standing up doing nothing and I let them go. If I saw they weren't going to produce enough to give me something and pay them too, they had to go. I looked at their attitude and it did not take long to see who could work for me. But I did have some good workers along with my sons.

I could have taken advantage of some of the people because they trusted me but that was not the man I was. I stayed calm, let nothing stop me and passed those same principles of being the best man with integrity on to my sons.

Alfred was going to high school and when they would get out of school he rushed out there to work. He saw a car he wanted, a green mustang. I think that car cost $1,200.00. He said, "Dad if you go get it I'll give you the money. I have it in the bank." When I got that money it was after he was killed. I closed his account. That was hard. It costs something to be a parent.

Family structure they got out here now is crazy, Family means something. Family and parenting is something serious!!

I told my wife when we got married, "If that doorbell rings at night don't you touch that door. Let me go. If anybody want to serve a bullet, let them put the first bullet in me. If somebody comes to stick up the church let them get me out of here first."

Family is so important. The many times I was in the hospital my wife and Shirley were right there with me. Even spending the night, they stayed right with me. They have been like that, all of my heart attacks, my strokes, right there.

Sharon takes care of my medication and when she was 16 years old, she said, "When you and mother get old I'll sell my house and move in with you and take care of you." She hadn't even started college and was working at Burger King on Schaefer and 9 Mile Road.

Mae Dee & Myself

Our family vacations were car trips to Mississippi. We got so much of a kick out of it. We would go once or twice a year in the summer and back for Christmas. Maybe sometimes I missed the trip and had only one a year but for sure one trip. We drove straight through because they didn't have any place for black people to spend the night and I didn't want to expose my family to prejudice. Some nights I couldn't drive over 15 miles an hour because they only had two lane highways. There were no expressways. The fog also made it hard to see, but I would just keep driving. My wife made a thermos of coffee and we had fried chicken and white bread. I would be driving and ask for a cup of coffee and that was the best coffee. I would ask for a chicken wing, a chicken leg, and a piece of bread and she would hand it to me. The coffee and chicken smelled so good in the car. I was strong enough to keep going and those were good times. My wife wouldn't go to sleep she would just sit there and keep me company. That was the best that was happening at that time. We would get back home to our parents, relax, start enjoying the family, stay one week or a few days or whatever, then head back home.

We would travel to Memphis, Tennessee to visit with my Mother who lived with my sister Easter there at my sister Frankie's two home family complex.

Easter, Mama & Frankie

What good times I had back then with my Mother and sisters.

My Father and Mother-in-law, Elder & Mother Lockhart were wonderful people. I remember one trip I took down there and my Mother-in-law said if I go catch some fish we would have fish for dinner.

Elder & Mother Lockhart

Sharon, Shirley, Linda and I went fishing in my father-in-law's pond and we caught a lot of fish. Feeling good walking back up to the house and saw Elder Lockhart, I showed him the fish, he said: "Good gracious you caught all of my good fish," our feathers dropped but we ate good fish for dinner.

My wife worked right along beside me and took care of the house and the money. She never worked for nobody until Alfred got killed in 1974. I wanted her to work outside the home because every time she opened that door she would see that bullet impression. I didn't want her to keep looking at that bullet impression

Mae Dee

in the front door. She went into real estate. That was just to get her out of the house. I was not asking her to put nothing in the house.

I'm hard on these guys now, courting these girls and don't have nothing in their pocket, can't even buy them a sandwich, mooching on the girls, telling them, you do this, getting the girl to set up something for the man. But right now for the average couple, it's hard to use that style. It takes almost two real energetic, smart people to marry to take things like they are now, stay together and build a home, because of the way things are set up and everything is so high and jobs are situated the way they are. But back in my day when you married the man took care of that family. I don't care what happened God made a way. We were all living about the same. It was hard times but that was how we were living.

Even with all of the things going on now in 2015, I believe that the man that God made me I could provide for my family of any size, without my wife working outside the home and putting her money in the house. My family would have food, transportation, a nice place to stay all that they need, God would help me provide. Paul said: *Not that I speak in respect of want: for I have learned, in whatsoever state I am, therewith to be content. I know both how to be abased, and I know how to abound: every where and in all things I am instructed both to be full and to be hungry, both to abound and to suffer need. I can do all things through Christ which strengtheneth me. Philippians 4:11-13.* Whatever state Paul was in he made himself content. There is a way of making it through the hard times if you put your trust in God.

We stayed on Mendota for a number of years and then we sold it and moved to St. Mary's.

ALFRED'S DEATH

On March 21, 1974 my baby son Alfred was murdered in my home. His Homegoing service was at our church, on March 26th. The Lord gave me the strength to preach his service, my text was "A Better Home". Several weeks after the death of my son, the man that I thought killed him came to my church every Sunday and would come up for prayer. I was able to pray for that man.

Alfred

I pointed him out to the police and from his actions and the things he said, I was judging him and I told the police that he just acted like a guy that did that. The police kept telling me, "Let us handle it. You will never be able to do it yourself." I pointed him out to the police and had him to sit beside me at one of the services for Alfred that week as the guy that I think did it. After the funeral service, every Sunday for several Sundays, I would ask God, "How am I going to pray for this man?" But God gave me grace to ask God to bless this man. I kept stepping over what I believed, that my baby boy was killed by you, I'm going to ask God to help you.

Time passed and my family had no peace because we did not know who took my baby son's life. I put the church on a fast and asked that they pray, that the person who killed my son, would come forward. One of them came forward. And it was not much longer after the fast, I found out the man I was praying for was not the man. The men who killed Alfred knew nothing about my family nor my son. It was just a random bunch looking for a home to rob.

After the death of my son, I wanted to move out of Detroit.

BELLEVILLE

When we came out here to purchase this land, my wife, didn't want the country nothing about the country, she was tired of the country. And her sister Bertha and brother-in-law Girty and both of us wanted some land out here so I talked up the notion and I talked him into buying some land together and that kind of turned her head this way. Then this property came up for sale, my brother-in-law James Jenkins, told me about it, I came out here and I bought it.

When we bought this property here, this was the only time I ever remember her giving a dime toward our estate. But I did not ask her. She volunteered. She said, "I'll tell you what, we'll just pay that off." She gave me $3,000.00 on this property. We moved to Belleville on December 28, 1976.

As a 95 year old man, I have much to be very happy about. I even think in terms of my ministry in traveling back and forth to various states. Seeing the hillsides the countrysides, animals and all of that which related to my life very much. So much so that I always desired to have those. God blessed me with the Belleville home where I could relate to my natural life. In that what I mean by relating to my natural life was, I would be able to have some of the things that I always from a child wanted, livestock and what have you. And I love to see natural life, especially rabbits, squirrels, deer and all of that, and I have been blessed with that, right here on the Belleville home. We have all of those animals like that, deer, squirrels, rabbits, possum, you name it, we have it here. Certainly I have enjoyed the pleasure of seeing them graze around occasionally. We have gone out hunting. I have killed squirrels, rabbits, brought them back here, cooked it and went back to my childhood days.

Not only that but, I found that it enhanced my family life with my

My Riding Club The Sunshine Riders

children, my grandchildren, and even with my church family. So many of the church family at times came out and enjoyed themselves. I'm the type of person that really enjoys seeing people happy. I would rather say, I'm really just a family man. The first Boone Family Reunion was at my home July 23-24, 1977. This was the beginning to a joyous reunion that we have had ever since.

I like to see everybody as a family and certainly those that even were blessed through the church family by coming out, riding the horses and when we set up even my riding club, the Sunshine Riders. I had about 16 members of my church that were part of that club, in which we had a lot of fellowship during rodeo entrances, state fair, occasionally doing picnics and also riding in the parades along with even some of my deacons, the members of the church and the some of the ministers. And life has been very beautiful.

And I think about my grandchildren, so many of them used to come and how

Riding at the Rodeo

Deacon Gray & Myself

they would ride and how they would play and it seemed like they enjoyed themselves. Especially one of my grandsons, Mark A. Moore, he was the first one of my grandsons that looked like at an early, early age started riding horses. He got so much of a kick out of it, and he enjoyed it so much, when I started my riding club I named my riding club after his horse, and I called our riding club The Sunshine Riders and his horse was named Sunshine. Of course that is where the name came

On Tracy

Mark & Myself with Sunshine

from. And of course in that it lasted for quite a few years, until later on we got to the place we didn't continue our club any further but we still have horses.

Some of the horses I had meant so much to me. I had several horses that I admired, I loved and like that, but I had at least three real special horses. And that was Rusty, Tracy and Skywalker. Those are my three favorite horses. I guess the top of the line would be Skywalker. That is the one I have now and I intend to maintain that horse as

long as he lives or I live or whatever. Because he was the last one I raised as a little baby colt up and he has been my horse ever since.

Now back to other things at the farm, I always loved, if I am not a good fisherman, I like to throw my hook out there and see the fish get a hold of it. I built me a pond out there and of course and even sometimes, I would come in from church at night, go out there and throw the pole in the water for a little bit, to get a few fish to bite my hook and like that. All of that was relaxing. And there were times I would get on my horse sometimes and ride him around the block, the roadside, the hillside, God would give me a message for the church.

So I am a happy man, 95 years old and God has blessed me not to be so sickly that my life was miserable. I have been able to maintain a happy life, a blessed life, and with my wife and

My Family

children and all of that, we have been able to maintain a family life, which I really thank God for.

And today I can say I thank God for the Belleville Home. It has enhanced me. And also to see, looking out the window now, back in the forest, seeing the trees out there, seeing my landscape and all of that, it makes me feel like this is natural life. So God blessed my life to this extent.

I can say today after 95 years of age, I'm very happy. I'm very happy. We have been able to

Life can be beautiful when God is in it.

have our flowers, our garden and all of those things and that is something always that I love. I love seeing things grow. I love agricultural life and I have been able to maintain a portion of that here.

So that is another thing where I can say that Belleville enhanced my life, because I enjoyed laboring with it. I built two fireplaces in my home. And I always love to just sit by the fireplace and get that good aroma that the wood in burning would send off and all of that to make me just go back in my childhood days and say, Lord I Thank You!

It is something I will never forget to leave the Lord out. Any good thing that happens that way, I have always found a way to say Lord I Thank You!

God bless every one of you. I hope what I am saying to you might make some of you say that Life is worth living. I can tell anybody today, life is worth living if you allow God to reign in your life. Life can be beautiful when God is in it.

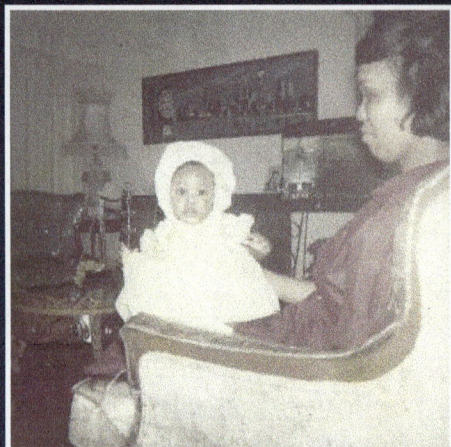

Mary holding our first
Grandchild, Kimberly Stacy
Boone

Mary & Myself with our
Great-Grandchildren the Kings

Mary & Myself with Shirley, Mark,
George & Sharon

4 Generations, Charles,
Charles A., Sheldon & Myself

Mary, Myself & Tony

My first Grandchild that is a Preacher!
Elder Mark A. Moore, Jr.

*My labor has not been in vain for my family, my children,
grandchildren, great-grandchildren, and those yet to be born.*

CHAPTER 6

ZION

EARLY DAYS IN THE MINISTRY

My wife's Uncle Leslie Ivy found out we were in Detroit, and he was going to Clinton Street Greater Bethlehem Temple and Zion was in our neighborhood. He told us about Zion, and Sister Richey and all of them were there and they just took us in like we were their children. That was real nice right then.

Elder Leaston had just started on Wyoming and 8 Mile Road in the basement church in Detroit, Michigan and was trying to grow. I was enthused about that and I wanted to see him with his dream and I wanted to go and grow with him. From my street on Mendota, I used to pick up so many children for Sunday School, I had them standing in the car, including Brother Stein David's daughter when she was four or five

Mae Dee & Myself

years old. We were a family as well as friends. I would cut the boys hair of the children of the other saints - the Glenns, Marshall and George, all of them.

Even back then Elder Leaston always had a vision for growing and doing something bigger. When he built the church and the saint's home, I was right there with him, wanting to see him see his dream come true. I was excited about trying to do that and I didn't see nobody helping him.

Bishop Hancock was the pastor at Clinton Street Greater Bethlehem Temple and over all of the churches in the area. I didn't know anything about him until after I met him. Elder Leaston used to be one of his members, so he made me acquainted with him after I became an assistant pastor going to the council. But I never wanted to move my membership to Clinton Street Bethlehem Temple. I wanted to help Elder Leaston.

I never thought that preaching was going to be part of my life. Because as far as getting up and thinking I was going to be a preacher I was shy, I didn't want it. I said it looked like God had to show me that He was going to have to kill me if I didn't do it. And for that cause I feel that God was taking me step by step to bring me to where I am.

After I got baptized in Jesus' Name and filled with the Holy Ghost, my mother was Baptist and my father was Methodist and all of them went after me. My mother cried and said, "You was good like you were what are you trying to get all of that for?"

My sister, Arizona Jenkins got saved. We were on Wyoming and 8 Mile Road in the basement church in Detroit. She was the first one of my family to get baptized in Jesus' Name and receive the gift of the Holy Ghost after me.

Arizona & Myself

After we moved to Reimanville in Ferndale, Elder Nebraska Edmonds out of West Virginia came and preached a revival at Zion. My mother broke down and she said I want to be saved and was the next one in my family that got baptized in Jesus' Name and got saved. I think Elder Richey baptized my mother in Jesus' Name. I was happy and just joy in my soul when I saw my mother come up to the front and said she wanted to get saved.

My sister, Arizona was the first sibling that got saved. From there came the completion of the whole thing. All of my sisters went down in Jesus' Name and got the Holy Ghost.

Elder Leaston had purchased the land on Reimanville across 8 Mile Road in Ferndale, but we had not started building yet. It took 1 ½ years to 2 years but we went to Reimanville, started there with a basement. We dug the basement, kept the basement then we built up from that. His vision was to go to Ferndale instead of finding some land in Detroit and I supported his vision.

I wanted to name my baby son, Alfred after Bishop Leaston. I wanted to name him Heardie

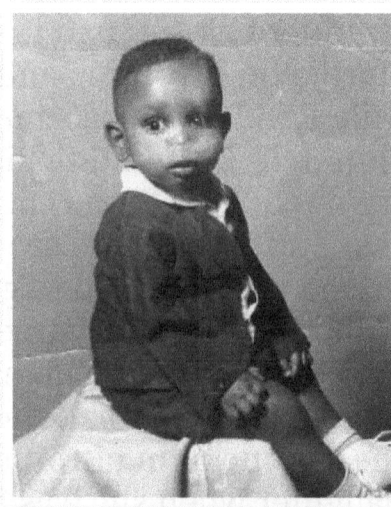

Baby Alfred

Alfred but my wife and family overruled me and I named him Alfred Heardie. Bishop Leaston was just so nice and taught me so much about holiness and the Apostolic Doctrine. Not in depths but just common sense and living right. That is why I just fell in love with Bishop Leaston and wanted to honor him. He always had a vision and wanted to build and do great things for God way back then and I wanted to help him all I could.

He built a Saints home called Zion's Rest Home that is still in existence today. I was right there with him and I was excited because I wanted to see his vision completed. He and I both wanted more than what was there. I always wanted more than what was in front of me. I had a pastor like me who wanted to see a greater vision and I wanted to be number one in helping him.

Bishop Hancock, Bishop Leaston & others

Back in that day when you said you were going to lay a cornerstone and the day came about, you always put some money in the cornerstone. If you say my name is Mattie Lou Johnson and I'm a member of this church you say well I'm going to put $5.00 in there. You just put it in there. Now I did that. I have money in that cornerstone, and others have money in there. I also put a few dollars in there for those who didn't have it. That cornerstone got some money in it and if some of those thugs knew that, they would take a sledgehammer and go in there and bust it up. Even though it is less than $100.00 in there.

When my brother-in-law Elder Rush Lockhart, Jr. laid the cornerstone at Zion Bishop Hancock was standing there with Bishop Leaston.

So back then we really worked but it was smooth. It wasn't a lot of stuff that you run into now. People were trying to build something for God, not for

Elder Lockhart, Myself, Bishop Halton, Bishop Leaston & Bishop Hancock

themselves. It was like Nehemiah we just got there and said you were going to build a house for the Lord. It only took 5-6 years to build the church and the rest home. And we didn't have any modern equipment.

God called me to preach the night I got the Holy Ghost. Brother O.B. Barnes said I preached in my sleep all night.

I knew it was on me even when I came back from the service. I didn't want that task. I fought it. I didn't want it. I didn't feel worthy. I didn't feel like I was a public speaker to get up before folks and do all of that. I felt inadequate for sure. I ran from it.

In 1949, while at the plant, God said, "Go to your pastor and tell him, I called you to preach." I knocked on the door and said, "Bishop I just come to tell you that The Lord has called me to preach." He said, "Preach?"

He dropped his head and said, "I'll talk to you later."

I went on. A little while later he came in the church tired, worked himself to death couldn't do Bible Class and I'm looking at him and he had the blackboard set up there and he was too tired and I was looking for him to get Bible Class started and he made the announcement. He hollered, "Ho, Ho! Elder Boone is going to preach for us tonight." I had never preached. That is how he brought me up.

The blackboard was set up for Bible Class and they never took it down. I got up there and had been practicing in my

mind, acting like T.S. Boone and different guys preaching over the air. I got so good at practicing it before I started preaching, I said when I get here I'm going to whoop and have a long whoop sound there. My first Sermon was "Lord, who shall abide." Psalm 15

Somebody called my wife and told her I was getting ready to preach. I don't know how she did it. But I looked in the back of the church and my wife and Ralph were coming in the door before I finished speaking.

After I finished preaching, I went and sat in the pulpit behind the blackboard and all you could see were my knees not my face. When I peeped around it I saw those young people including Ellen Shorter laughing at me. I would rather be dead when I got through with that sermon.

During that night, after we got home, my wife gave me her position. "If you are going to preach, go ahead. I don't want you to be a jackleg preacher." She still hasn't told me 69 years later if I have gotten past being a jackleg preacher.

It did not help that others were doubting whether or not I could preach. It seemed like the people were against me preaching. You ain't ready to preach. You ain't praying like you ought to. But that next day God shut all of them up.

Mother Heard saw me in the store the next day and chastised me. "You didn't let the Lord use you. You let the Lord use you. Tonight is Missionary Night I want you to preach. Let the Lord use you. Do it."

Mother Heard

Now this was after Bible Class and I just got over the hurt of that. Now I got to preach Thursday night. She said do it and I got up there. Galatians 5:1 hit my mind, *Stand fast therefore in the liberty wherewith Christ hath made us free, and be not entangled again with the yoke of bondage.* God anointed me so I enjoyed it. That was a life saver for my ministry. If I hadn't come through that time I would have been through with it. I was just through with the pulpit. The way Mother Heard did me, God used me. I'm going to tell you. I felt better preaching that sermon than just about any other sermon I preached, I felt free, I was anointed, God gave me the word, He made it real short and quick and people responded.

I continued doing anything that needed to be done at Zion. Lawn, landscaping, cutting the grass at Bishop Leaston's house, building things. I would carry money for him to go up to 8 Mile Road to get people and pay them to help him when I couldn't be there to lay block. I was the Sunday School Superintendent and the driver. I used to pick them all up on the school bus Ellen Cunningham, Sister Kelly and her family and others in the neighborhood. I was Superintendent for a few years, Deacon for a while then made Assistant Pastor. I would do anything to serve God and help my pastor.

We had service every night except Saturday and I was appointed to be the Assistant Pastor so after working my three jobs I wanted to be there for every single one.

Monday, Prayer and Tarrying
Tuesday, Young People
Wednesday, Bible Class
Thursday, Missionary
Friday, Saint's Meeting
Sunday, Sunday School, Morning Worship, 4:00 p.m. afternoon service Sometimes we would go to another church for Missionary Service back at Zion at 8:00 p.m. for night service.

I would get up Sunday at 4:00 a.m. to get that old bus warmed, to go pick up children, crank it, warm up plugs and all. Sometimes it would take an hour to crank it. That means sometimes the carburetor would have water frozen in it and I would light paper, warm that up, let that gas out, let some real gas come in, go and crank it. Sometimes I would have to warm up the plugs. It was a lot of things. My wife would be over on the west side and I would get Elder Richey after Sunday School to go pick her up and bring her to church. We would take the bus and go back there. Things were rough then.

I remember before the licensing of the automobile drivers was as strict as they now are, I taught most of the mothers with the permission of their husbands and other people in the church how to drive and be responsible for their cars.

Wanting to improve myself in the academic world as well as wanting to get a better knowledge of the Bible, I enrolled in the Detroit Bible Institute and I attended the Aenon Bible School, whose doctrine is strictly Apostolic-Pentecostal.

I was ordained in January 1961, by the late Bishop Samuel N. Hancock at the Clinton Street Greater Bethlehem Temple Church in Detroit, Michigan. I served as a District Elder in the Michigan State Council of the Pentecostal Churches of the Apostolic Faith, Inc. and I was a Field Worker. I was elected Assistant Council Chairman. Two years later, I was elected as Chairman of the Council.

Bishop Lee, Mother Tucker, Mother Mitchell, Myself & others

CHAPTER 7

NEW LIBERTY APOSTOLIC FAITH CHURCH

LEAVING ZION AND BECOMING A PASTOR

I have always been zealous for souls. Not that I wanted to be the front man, I just was always burdened and looked out for souls. I just wanted to get out of Michigan and hoped God would settle me in the south because I had a burden for Mississippi. I wanted to leave Michigan. I was tired of Michigan.

The Ratcliffs and all of them came in and got baptized at Zion and they lived down there in Meridian, Mississippi. I went down there and would do revivals and preach and other people would get saved down there. It was a flourishing area and I believed I would do better and I wanted to get out of Michigan.

I was in Muskegon, Michigan in revival and closed my service off in October and headed south and said, "Lord I want you to give me a place in the south."

I didn't get back until January. I had my people to meet me down there and we had Christmas down there. I asked God to solidify and substantiate me in the south. I went to Fort Wayne, Indiana and they gave me a church that was falling apart with a congregation of 20 members. I came on back to Detroit.

My sister that died in 2014, Myrtle Fears, lived in Brownstown, moved out there and they had built up a little community out there. I said to my pastor, Bishop Leaston, "On the nights when we don't have service, I would like to have prayer and teach Bible Class and somebody out there will get saved." I started in her living room.

He encouraged me, supported me and gave me permission and told me to go ahead, to go out there and start a work. I started baptizing in Jesus' Name and people began getting the Holy Ghost and that church began to come together. I started New Liberty out there. I was driving through Palmer Woods and saw a church named New Liberty and God just fascinated and fastened my mind on New Liberty.

After while I rented a building, started a Sunday School, got me a piano got me some lumber and made some benches and put them together. I had opening day, put all that stuff in the building and Sister Mitchell, Sister Glenn, Sister Richey and all of them came and filled that place up.

I went by the hospital to see Elder Joe Harris. He said, "A long time ago the Lord laid that very spot on my heart. The Lord is going to deliver me from all of this." I said, "When He does you will have a church." When he got out of the hospital I turned it over to him.

New Liberty's formulating meeting was held in Elder Frank Stanley's home with 23 chartered members, on Saturday, January 4, 1964.

Mother Heard told me about the House of Joy, an old beauty shop at 13723 Linwood. It was vacant and I put $200.00 on it and that is how we got it. Our first service was held there Friday, January 10, 1964. My first message was, "I will publish the name of the Lord." *Give ear, O ye heavens, and I will speak; and hear, O earth, the words of my mouth. My doctrine shall drop as the rain, my speech shall distil as the dew, as the small rain upon the tender herb, and as the showers upon the grass: Because I will publish the name*

of the Lord: ascribe ye greatness unto our God. Deuteronomy 32:1-3. The first Sunday, January 12, 1964, Message I preached was "I will look unto the hills from whence cometh my help, my help cometh from the Lord." *I will lift up mine eyes unto the hills, from whence cometh my help. Psalm 121:1*

We stayed there for one year. When the Lord blessed us and we outgrew that, Elder Richey found 2330 Fenkell. We bought that property where we stayed approximately for three years as our membership grew. The first Secretary of the church was Evangelist Lovora J. Walker and Brother Bob Brown was the first Treasurer. Deacon Nathan Walker was the first Chairman of the Deacon Board. We formed our auxiliaries there: Missionary Department, with the first Usher Board Chairman, Mother Eva Dowdell, Sharon Boone and Brenda Howard as the first two ushers.

2330 Fenkell Pulpit

Harvest Time was a dream that Evangelist Walker had because I had a landscaping business and I only worked

2330 Fenkell Pulpit

My 1st Deacon Board

Harvest Time

in the spring and summer. She said it would be good to have a harvest service. So she asked my permission if they could start what they called Harvest Time.

November every year they started bringing in food and all of that kind of stuff and bringing it in to go through the winter. It was a tremendous help. She kept going with it for so long that every time there was harvest service, she announced that the saints should get up and give until the grass turns green and then he can go back to work. I said that don't sound good. I interceded enough for them to call it Appreciation because they were giving from their hearts for the good of their pastor and his family.

I been tested when it comes down to whether I am a man or whether I am a mouse but I choose to be a man even today. Some things I just always want to be all man. I don't want to be no mouse or nothing like that. Be a man or else - I heard the Lord say when He was looking for a man to stand with Jeremiah for the people of God: *Run ye to and fro through the streets of*

Jerusalem, and see now, and know, and seek in the broad places thereof, if ye can find a man, if there be any that executeth judgment, that seeketh the truth; and I will pardon it.
Jeremiah 5:1

I always stood firm and never backed down from anything. We moved to 8425 Fenkell, our first service there was October 4, 1968 and we have been there ever since.

I had this to happen to me in the early 1970's. A guy came into New Liberty and Mother Lee and all of them got him on the altar and started tarrying with him. He said, "I didn't come in for this. I came in to get some money and they got me down here on my knees," and he pulled out a gun. I said, "No, you've got to go."

I got in front of him and was between the pistol and the people. He never touched me and I never touched him. He put that gun on me and I said, "You got to go. Let's go! Let's go! Let's go!" He backed down the aisle, with that gun on me. My baby son, Alfred was about 16, trying to get around me to attack the fellow. I pushed my son Alfred back. I just felt like he was going to shoot me when he stepped out the door. From the time we left the altar I was expecting to get shot. He remained about three feet from me. When he stepped out the door he put the gun in his pocket and took off. *The power of the Holy Ghost drove him out of the church.* I just went back in and completed the service. I was protecting my church, my spiritual and natural family.

When I think back over my life, I think in terms of why I was so hesitant about trying to take up the ministry. But in that I find that because it's a great task, it's not anything that we make up ourselves. It's something that has been mandated by God and I've been of this conviction that what God mandates that is what He means to be done.

I was thinking about my ministry and coming up through the many years and all of that, and of course I thought about it before I entered into it. I knew it was something heavy but I didn't really know what it was. When I began to exercise and interest myself in the ministry, I found this. That it is something that we've got to be serious about. It is something we are going to have to give an account for.

In My Pulpit 70's

I was even thinking about the 5 Fold Ministries. The 5 Fold Ministries is something that must be for the saints to be perfected. If it is not carried out right, somebody is going to come up missing perfection. And certainly from that standpoint, I look at it from this standpoint, that it is a thing that must be done according to the Spirit of God.

Again back to the 5 Fold Ministries when we look at all of it, I notice there, it says that one of the 5 Fold Ministries is to Pastor. I look at that from the standpoint of what we might find in our everyday living and everyday life.

We go to these great automobile plants, they have men all lined up for certain things about the cars. You have people that work on the transmission. You have the mechanic. You have the electrician. You have other men that are tactful for cars. And of course in the midst of that you have a Shop Foreman and he is over all of them. That doesn't necessarily mean that he has to be the best but he has to have enough of all of it to know when to stamp his signature on the product for the customers to be happy with.

So in that, I'm looking at the 5 Fold Ministries, and I have always felt that a pastor, if one is called to pastor they should be able to conduct at least one or two revivals every year at their own church as a pastor. I heard out of the book of Hebrews where the Lord says: *Obey them that have the rule over you, and submit yourselves: for they watch for your souls, as they that must give account, that they may do it with joy, and not with grief: for that is unprofitable for you. Hebrews 13:17*

For that cause, I feel this. That every pastor ought to have enough of the 5 Fold Ministries, when a person comes in and says that they are an evangelist, the pastor should know enough about evangelism to know whether or not this is an evangelist. If they say they are a prophet, the pastor should have enough to know whether or not they are a false prophet or whether they are a man or woman of God.

And I was looking at all of that, I feel that is what makes me feel that nobody could do a better revival at your own church than you. But I do feel that dedicating yourself to the Lord and praying for God to help you, that is one of the best revivals that you could conduct at your own church. If that 5 Fold Ministry is in you and you go forward as God says, I feel like that is the most impactful revival you are going to have at your church.

And since I see that, I always said to myself, I was going to do a revival. Over the Apostolic Assemblies of Christ, I tell my pastors, I want to see every one of you pastors, I feel that if you pray right God is going to give it to you. Do your one revival at your own church a year. And I have had pastors come up and they have been very successful in it.

Going back to the 5 Fold Ministries again it is a must, Paul said for the perfecting of the saints, for the edifying of the body of Christ, till we all come into the unity and the knowledge of the Son of God. *And he gave some, apostles; and some, prophets; and some, evangelists; and some, pastors and teachers; For the perfecting of the saints, for the work of the ministry, for the edifying of the body of Christ: Till we all come in the unity of the faith, and of the knowledge of the Son of God, unto a perfect man, unto the measure of the stature of the fulness of Christ: Ephesians 4:11-13*

For that cause I'm very serious in my heart I feel that every pastor somewhere in their pastoral time should take off and do a church revival at their own church.

In the early 1970's it is something about God I noticed in my ministry. God laid it on my heart to do a revival.

> *For that cause I'm very serious in my heart I feel that every pastor somewhere in their pastoral time should take off and do a church revival at their own church.*

God had a young man out of Arkansas, Brother Tenolia Davidson, who was only 17 years old, to come in and unite here with our church. He was a very fine young man, very faithful. I made him a deacon and he worked hard and everybody loved him.

During this revival, that 17 year old young man was so instrumental and worked so hard with me in that revival. He was driving the van, going out into the hedges and the highways sounding the alarm about the revival. There were 65 souls baptized in Jesus' Name and filled with the Holy Ghost that got saved in that one revival, which was less than two weeks. I think it must have been maybe about 10 or 11 days of service that we had. But 65 souls got saved, filled with the Holy Ghost in that revival, not weeks or months later but during that revival. Some of them died and we planted them in the earth but I'm looking for them to rise on that great getting up morning.

So I feel, it is my conviction, that if we say we will pastor, we ought to say we are going to evangelize our church. I don't think there is a better evangelist that can come into your church than that portion that God gives you to evangelize your own church with.

During my pastoral life I appreciated many things God used me in and He only gets the glory in these things. There were many miracles I saw wrought by prayer, I'm here to testify that God can, I'm here to testify that God is a healer, that God is a deliverer,

and all He wants is somebody that will live right and be down to earth and down to business when it comes down to their salvation.

During my 51 years of pastoral service, I experienced quite a few things, learned quite a bit about the Lord in my endeavors. I've seen the handiwork of God work in many instances, especially at my own church. I've seen the dead raised, I've seen the sick healed, I've seen miracles worked right in my congregation.

I remember one occasion where one of my great members, Brother Connie L. Foster, was in an accident and the doctors all declared that he was dead and never would be able to come back to life again anymore as he should. And I went in and told them I wanted to pray for him. The doctors stepped back and looked at me as good as to say, go ahead and pray for him. They were very sarcastic. They acted like they wanted me to pray, but at the same time, they didn't believe God was going to move. I had to pray for Brother Foster because I wanted God to perform a miracle because He is a miracle working God and I wanted people to see that He is still performing miracles. You hear people talking about church and holiness is this and this, and it ain't no signs, I ain't never believed in that. It ought to be some signs in the church, God said: *And these signs shall follow them that believe; In my name shall they cast out devils; they shall speak with new tongues; They shall take up serpents; and if they drink any deadly thing, it shall not hurt them; they shall lay hands on the sick, and they shall recover. Mark 16:17-18.* And I am a believer, don't tell me I'm not.

I wanted these people to see a miracle and know that the God that I serve answered prayer. And I'm here to testify today, that the night I prayed for him, he received life back in his body and lived 15 years longer, went about doing his regular routine of life. In fact I made him the chairman of the National Usher Board in the Apostolic Assemblies of Christ and the Lord restored his body back. Many parts of his body that they said never would function again, but God put that back together. I saw that for myself. And for verification of that Brother Connie L. Foster said to the doctors, every one of you all that knew I was dead, I would like for you just to leave your name with me. And there are six Doctors names that signed a statement and said this man was dead when the minister prayed for him. But now he is back to life again.

Those types of things, I feel like God wants the church to be involved in. It is too much of this stuff about double standards, and it don't take all of this. And I am of this opinion, that we are saying it

I knew it was not God's will for me to remain as active pastor forever and I began to seek God for His will, His timing and His choice for a successor.

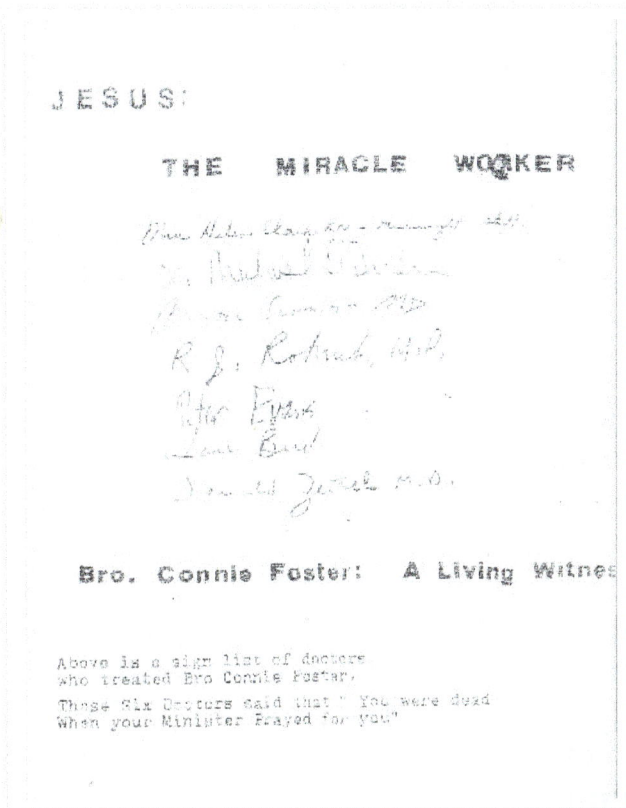

Doctors signed this Statement

don't take all of this, I think we are going to find many people are going to find that it took more than what they did in order for the Lord to say well done.

The burden and zeal I have for souls manifested itself again in 1964 when the Lord led me to establish New Liberty Apostolic Faith Church. We went through transitions and the growth process with the Lord leading us every step of the way. Many who started with us have gone to their reward. But never has there been a shortage of God's presence leading us and His anointing to keep us moving forward. Souls have continued to come and be saved, filled and delivered. I knew it was not God's will for me to remain as active pastor forever and I began to seek God for His will, His timing and His choice for a successor.

He answered my prayers and sent the young man to stand at the helm of New Liberty. I am confident based on his attitude, conduct, treatment of God's people and his hunger for God's will in his life, that he is the best choice. February 19, 2014 Orientation for Impartation was held and Sunday, January 11, 2015, I passed the Mantle.

With this young man at the helm of New Liberty Apostolic Faith Church, I am confident that my legacy will continue for years to come with District Elder J.O. Rasul, this humble, obedient, anointed young man leading the way.

Anointing my Successor

Praying for my Successor

My Successor

District Elder & Sister J.O. Rasul
& Myself

For 51 Years I Pastored some Wonderful Saints

I hope that my life and ones I'm dealing with, they will pass the legacy on. That is my hope.

Mother Thompson & Myself

Elder Lee & Myself

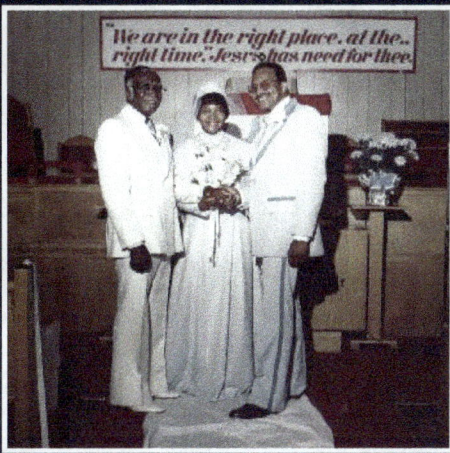
Deacon & Sister Williams
Wedding

Mother Brooks & Mother Blanding

Mother Dowdell & Myself

Deacon Kilgore & Mary

Mary & Myself with
Minister & Evangelist
Henderson

Mary with Mother Brooks, Mother Davis,
Mother Lee, Mother Blanding,
Mother Bennett, Mother Foster &
Mother Thompson

Mother Davis & Myself

Deacon Kilgore & Myself

Sister Kilgore, Shirley & Myself

Rhonda & Mary

Mary, Myself, Sister Moultrie, Mark,
George & Sharon

Mary & Myself with our Deacon Board

Mary & Myself with our daughter, Linda

Mary & Myself with
Mother Lee

Mary & Minister
Winn

Mary & Myself with Mother Williams, Mother Brown,
Mother Abner & Mother Stanifer

Evangelist Sanders & Myself

Elder Brown, Sister Rasul, Evangelist Dawn,
Sister Sharisee & Sister Ellaree

My Trustee Board

Bishop Mahone & Myself

Mother Lee & Elder Sanders

Mary & Myself with Sister Evans

Mary & Mother Briscoe

My Deacon Board

My labor has not been in vain for New Liberty Apostolic Faith Church

CHAPTER 8

━━━━━ ∽ ━━━━━

APOSTOLIC ASSEMBLIES OF CHRIST, INC.

I didn't share it with the church at that time but I always wanted to move forward. I didn't have the organization in mind. I wanted to have a nice big church. That was my focus. After God gave me the vision for the Apostolic Assemblies of Christ, much of what I had in mind, for New Liberty was birthed in the Apostolic Assemblies of Christ. I got on the field and got other states and other countries in mind and didn't go forward with that. Some working with me didn't prove faithful so it was a setback for the growth of my church. But we were able to maintain and we are doing well now.

Bishop Lee & Myself

But those things I look at as one of the ways that God has us going through various things and letting us know, "I'm with you."

Bishop Willie Lee, the Presiding Bishop of the Pentecostal Churches of the Apostolic Faith, Inc. in 1965 ordained me as a Bishop.

March 20, 1970 is when I founded The Apostolic Assemblies of Christ. The first meeting was at my church in Detroit with seven churches in three states.

In attendance were:
- New Liberty, Detroit, Michigan - Bishop G.M. Boone, Pastor The Mother Church of the Apostolic Assemblies of Christ
- Bishop Virgil H. Oates, Port Huron, Michigan
- Elder Willie J. Duncan, Muskegon, Michigan

- Elder Fred Majors, Dayton, Ohio
- Pastor Parilee Mitchell, Milan, Michigan
- Elder James Ward, Nashville, Tennessee
- Elder Nebraska Edmonds, Detroit, Michigan

Mother Mitchell

I give Mother Mitchell real credit for the name. I had a name. Bishop Oates had a name. Elder Edmonds had a name. Mother Mitchell said, "Why don't we just bring these names together?" she said Apostolic Assemblies of Christ.

We went through quite a few changes. Some said it wouldn't happen, because there was nothing to make it happen with. Others said we don't need another Apostolic organization and this one would never get off the ground. Some of them even said, we would never get our nose out of the dust and it wasn't of God. One even came into my pulpit and looked me in the eye and said, Oh no, the splinter has splint the splinter. A bunch of them came together and inquired about what seminary had I studied at, what degrees I had. One of

the bishops spoke up and said, this fellow is just a man with good mother wit and was used by God to get his organization going. It took me back to the Word of God. *Then stood there up one in the council, a Pharisee, named Gamaliel, a doctor of the law, had in reputation among all the people. . .and said unto them, Ye men of Israel, take heed to yourselves what ye intend to do as touching these men. . . Refrain from these men, and let them alone: for if this counsel or this work be of men, it will come to nought: But if it be of God, ye cannot overthrow it; lest haply ye be found even to fight against God. Acts 5:33-39*

One of the brethren said to the group about the Apostolic Assemblies of Christ. If it is of God it will stand. If it is not it will fall. And we with God's help 45 years later are still standing.

My Wife

All of this was a great challenge for me. It hurt my wife so much because she was watching me go through all of the bickering and at one point, was so hurt because I was so hurt, asked me why don't you just leave it alone? But God never let me faint. That is why my scripture is: *"Having therefore obtained help of God, I continue unto this day..." Acts 26:22*

1st National Convention

God gave me a Vision and I asked God to give me a People for the Vision.

I was blessed to organize many Councils, Michigan State Council, Central District Council, Southern District Council, Illinois/Indiana District Council, Eastern District Council, Gulf State Council, California State Council, Tennessee Carolina Council, Texas State Council, Mountain State Council, West Virginia Carolina Council, Hawaii State Council, Northern California Council, Wisconsin State Council. I have three chartered churches with me today.

In the beginning, we didn't have lawyers, no real businessmen in our midst, no CPAs, didn't have a lot of things that I have now, but as of today we have the organization set up beautifully. As far as IRS, I've got Bookkeepers, capable people, Attorney, CPAs, Lieutenant Colonel, Businessmen, and all are diehards as far as standing for the Apostolic truth, so I don't worry about it.

My nephew, Bishop Cooper is Chairman of the Steering Committee and we are looking good for what we have accomplished.

Later I became a part of the Apostolic World Christian Fellowship. Some people were against that and some said don't even put him in as an organization just let him be an independent church. Bishop Rowe asked me how many churches did I have because I had to have a minimum of 12 churches, and I had almost doubled that then. Since then I have exceeded that quite a bit more. Since that time the Apostolic World Christian Fellowship has grown beyond 250 Apostolic organizations throughout the world system. I know it is over 250 because the last time I met them I met that.

Bishop Samuel Smith the Chairman of The Apostolic World Christian Fellowship came up with the idea that the one that was the longest served Presiding Bishop of an Apostolic organization would be honored by them with the Apostolic Torch. On May 16, 2012, I humbly accepted that torch and it is now on my desk at New Liberty Apostolic Faith Church. Who would have thought, that the little boy that was raised during the depression, would serve as the longest served Presiding Bishop in the history of the Apostolic Movement?

Holding the Apostolic Torch

Bishop Davis & Myself

Bishop Casper Cohens, Sr. of Emmanuel Apostolic Church in Greenville, South Carolina, was a great asset to the forward movement of the organization. One of his members, then Brother Johnny L. Davis was a lay member of Emmanuel Apostolic Church in Greenville, South Carolina. His pastor, then Elder Casper Cohens, Sr. saw his potential and asked me to ordain him to be a deacon. I ordained him at the National Convention as deacon and his commitment to God and the organization led me to move him from one elevation to another. I stepped him up to District Elder, Suffragan Bishop now to full Bishop. Not only that, now he is Parliamentarian and one of our businessmen to the organization that we have on our Steering Committee.

In 1971, the Lord led me to anoint the hands of my youngest daughter, Shirley. He told me she was going to be the musician for New Liberty. She did not know how to play a piano or organ and even though she was taking lessons, she did not want to play. On the 4th Sunday morning in July, 1971 the musician did not come to church on time. I walked to the back of the sanctuary and told Shirley what God showed me, "Baby girl, get on that organ." She went to the organ and played like she had been playing for 20 years.

My greatest hands on help with the Apostolic Assemblies of Christ is my daughter Shirley. She ignited more, gave more assistance from the least to the greatest. God anointed her, she is an organizer and she is courageous. Not only that, she loves the Apostolic Movement, Loves God and her daddy. If it had not been for her, the organization wouldn't be where it is today. The Lord has through our endeavor supplied all of our needs according to His riches in Glory.

Shirley & Myself

Who would have thought that the anointing of her hands to play the organ for the church, would lead to her hands being the hands that would help shape, grow and serve the Apostolic Assemblies of Christ. I did not know. She did not know. But God knew. That was what He really had in mind when He told me to anoint her hands. He was preparing her for the greater work to come and knew I would need my daughter's help. So God got her ready.

I never asked Shirley to do this or do that. When I was running from state to state, she would get under that wheel and hit the highway whether it was 2 hours or 18 hours driving. She would drive all night and day in all kinds of weather.

While traveling and building the Apostolic Assemblies of Christ I bought a new car every two years because we did so much driving.

When I traveled, I always left Michigan with enough money in my pocket to get there and get back home. I did not travel expecting anybody to pay my way back or pay for my food. I took care of myself. I did not go in the south land to get somebody to give me an offering to get back home.

My wife wanted for nothing when I was gone. When I was building the Apostolic Assemblies of Christ and my daughter was traveling with me, my wife, Mother Mae Dee Boone stayed home and took care of the home front while I took care of the country. I did not leave my wife broke or not having enough money. No bill collectors or anybody came to evict my wife who was still at home. Light bill, gas bill, phone bill all were paid up in advance. I left her set.

New Liberty Church did not want for anything either. I had a devoted Assistant Pastor, Elder Paul Lee who took care of New Liberty while I was traveling. Elder and Sister Lee's untimely tragic deaths in the same automobile accident, put me in bad shape. I felt like I was getting on the highway but I didn't have a brand new car. And if I had a new car I had a spare tire with no air. I had to see what God was going to do and how He was going to do it.

All night I rode in the car from state to state building God's organization. In the southland where some people were castaways and felt like they were nobody, didn't ever feel like they would be anybody, but back woods people - those are some of the ones God sent me to shepherd. I went in the south and touched many of these people.

I did not go down there like I was a king. I was humble, loving and caring and caught the heart of many of these people. I didn't go there and stay in a penthouse hotel. I would stay in their homes and some of the offerings were the food they served me. One week I ran a revival at a church, preached my heart out and I only received $30.00. They said, "You can look at him and tell that he don't need no money." I went in the rain, in the snow, in the fog. I have no regrets.

I buried I don't know how many of my pastors. I actually paid for homegoing services when some of the pastors died without insurance money for burial, and I was there for the membership. I covered my people.

I went down to Tumusooma, Mississippi and stayed with a couple. They knew I was coming and the husband and wife were both working. I did not know how to cook and there was nothing cooked in the house so I had to go to the store to get some cheese and crackers so I would have something to snack on. There was no heat in the house and before the husband left for work that morning, I got a surprise! He said, "I have a tree up on the side of the hill. I have two mules in the stable. One has a flopped ear. That one is mean so get the other one, take him up to the tree, cut the tree down and chop up the wood for some heat for the house." I took the mule, pulled the whole logs down to the house, cut it up and stacked it up and that was the firewood that kept heat in that house. Everybody had heat all week long because of my labor. I was there for a week and his wife cooked dinner when she came home. I remember the house was also full of cats. But I was on a mission from God.

My motto in building the Apostolic Assemblies of Christ when I was going in the south was "Everybody is somebody." And that has been proven repeatedly over these 45 years. When I was building in the south the ones that felt like they were nobody, I made them feel like they were somebody. To this day some of the ones that felt like they were nobody are bishops and carrying the organization.

We sure saw that back in the day when I was building the organization. Some of them had no education, some could not read or write but I worked with them. Some have gone on to be with the Lord but when they died they were somebody. I went after the ones nobody else wanted because of the love

I have for downfallen humanity.

November, 1980 I spent Thanksgiving with my Father and Mother-in-law in Oxford, Mississippi. It was a wonderful Thanksgiving. My wife,

Standing on Elder & Mother Lockhart's Porch

Shirley, John Walker and some more saints were with me. We left there and drove to Carthage, Mississippi to Elder Mink Whittington's Church and I organized the Southern District Council. Mother Eva Dowdell chartered a bus for my church and they went down. During that Council, Mother Imogene Washington was healed, she left her crutch down there and two of my grandchildren, Todd and Tiffany, received the Holy Ghost.

God sent me Bishop Paul O. Jones, Jr. to work by my side. In 1991, I appointed him as the Co-Assistant Presiding Bishop.

Bishop Jones & Myself

Looking back over such a Great Organization that God allowed me to be the founder of, my heart is overwhelmed. I appreciate the Lord for preserving my life, and all of the accomplishments He has allowed us to obtain. I am thankful for all of the many jewels that God has allowed to work faithfully along side of me.

The Late Assistant Presiding Bishop and Mother Oates, as we started out together. I honor all of the many saints that

Bishop & Mother Oates

have gone on to be with the Lord that helped me to get where I am today.

It had been a bother in my spirit concerning where the organization would end up if God called me home but as always, God brought everything in position. Everything is looking good. Looking at the Apostolic Assemblies of Christ, it went through quite a bit of crisis with people but now things are looking good.

When I obeyed God and established the Apostolic Assemblies of Christ, Inc. in 1970 there were a lot of things that changed for New Liberty Apostolic Faith Church, my family and myself. I realized dreams and plans I had for another purpose were actually meant for the Apostolic Assemblies of Christ.

Bishop Sorrells & Myself

Passing the Mantle

God has used this organization to bring His message of hope and salvation all over the world. There is more than me in this plan.

I consult God before any decision. However, with a serious decision, especially when it involves New Liberty Apostolic Faith Church or the Apostolic Assemblies of Christ, I consult God for direction and confirmation. After much prayer, fasting, waiting and seeking God for direction, I listened and received my answer and confirmation.

It was in my spirit to appoint someone to be my successor for the organization. I asked God for confirmation of who it should be. I could have made the direct appointment but I wanted to be in God's Divine Will and I secretly promised Him that

The most important thing to me at this stage in my life is that my legacy will be upheld, continued and built upon for the next generations.

whoever He saw fit to be elected, would be my choice.

Friday, July 27, 2012, at 42 years and going strong, I passed the Mantle of the Apostolic Assemblies of Christ to Bishop Donald Sorrells, D.D. who served under me faithfully for over 30 years. The most important thing to me at this stage in my life is that my legacy will be upheld, continued and built upon for the next generations, according to the Divine Will of God. Passing the mantle to Bishop Donald Sorrells, gives me that peace and in 2015, Bishop Sorrells, I salute you. I thank you for being the man God has chosen, the Apostolic Assemblies of Christ elected and the man that I confirmed, who will lead us into the next level of building and growth.

Anointing my Successor

Praying for my Successor

LEGACY

My flesh and blood legacy - I want to see some of them who are babies today so determined that my legacy will be respected that they will stand as a pillar or post down the road. I'm looking for that.

My spiritual legacy - I'm looking at other members who don't have to be a Boone. Someone born there as a babe in Christ, I would like to see them standing right there as the oldest deacon or a preacher. I want them to say, "Don't worry about this, I've got it covered."

That is my dream. I said to one of my Great Grand's. I walked up to him and said, "I'm looking for you to be a pillar and a post in this church. I'm looking for that. That is one of my requests to you." God will give it to me. He can do it. He can be that pillar and that post. I long to see things of that nature.

Pillar means permanent people in the church. Post means standing in place supporting the pillars of the church. What would I do without their work? Without people of their integrity? To work on building the kingdom and bringing in souls? Some of the church is under physical construction now and in short I look forward to the completion of the construction. I want people who will say, "Don't worry about any of this. We will take care of everything." I want good people who will see projects all the way through even after I'm gone. Then that makes me feel like when the Rapture takes place here comes New Liberty. Here comes the Apostolic Assemblies of Christ.

As you all know this book has to do with my legacy not just because it is me, but because of God. I'd like for this to be on record, that is why I don't mind investing in this to be on someone's mind down the road.

Through it all God can help us. My hard times have been reflected here. My upbringing is here. My struggle being in the church has been reflected and it is a signal that somebody can make it. That is one of the things I'm looking at this for. Take me now and look here.

I hope that my life and ones I'm dealing with, they will pass the legacy on. That is my hope.

My church and my organization, the standard and all of the principles that we try to live up to. I want it where somebody will keep the legacy and keep it going.

I may have some devils at my church but they all love and respect me. All of them are not devils. I am not talking about all of them. I have some beautiful, saved, lovely people. But you are always going to have a Judas in your midst. If I didn't I wouldn't have nothing to work for.

I am enjoying telling this story. I am enjoying reminiscing about all of this because the memories bring back happy times and shows me how far God has brought me.

I have Children in so many different states and I wish it was so me and my driver, Elder Sanders could just go and see this one and that one. I'm not too much for foreign travel just give me the good old United States where I've had churches.

Elder Sanders & Myself

That is why I am so happy about what I see at my church now and the new pastor that came out of the street under my ministry. He is a good preacher. Loves me. Used to be one of my Amour Bearers. People like his preaching

My Successor

and all of the churches in Detroit when I began to start counseling him and his wife about pastoring, we would go out for breakfast and others would see us and tell me, "Bishop, you got your man here." Everybody likes him. I said, "Lord you are telling me something." He has taken over New Liberty.

I'm enthused about this thing. Felt too much of it. Saw the Lord do so many things. I want to see what else He's got. I'm about to believe that He will do anything He can do and I believe He will do anything if I ask Him in the right type of position. I feel the same way. I believe it just like the word says. I don't put nothing on God He didn't do.

If we do what we are supposed to do, God will do what He is supposed to do. If we reach the conditions that God set which are:

Have the right faith to believe in God and the reason for what we want.

Don't let it be something for the flesh, for His glory let our endeavor be to glorify God - Not my will, but your will be done.

Glorify God not the flesh.

We ask God a lot of things about our desire and what we want to do.

But keep His will in your mind.

Let me be found in the center of your will.

When I passed the mantle to my organization and my church, I knew I was in the will of God.

I feel like when I tell my story, to the glory of God, I am in the will of God.

I feel like I have presented a legacy to show my natural children, my spiritual children and all who are as many as the Lord Our God Shall Call, the way to work, live and serve God.

All that I have told you in this volume did happen. I took great care to tell it exactly as it happened so as not to offend My Lord who has blessed me nor anyone else. In that same spirit, as I come to this point I leave you with the blessing God has given as a direct result of my labor.

I set out to lay a foundation for my walk with God and my family. It took time, blood, sweat, tears, toil, prayer, obedience, waiting, patience, faith, grace, mercy, understanding, strength, courage, wisdom. Most of all it took trust in God and time. It took my time to line up with God's time that I could never see. It took listening for God's voice and when I could not hear His voice, I walked by faith. Had I walked by sight I would have fainted. He took a long time and poured so much through me to build this foundation but now I know why it took so long. There is so much resting on this foundation.

My labor has not been in vain for the Apostolic Assemblies of Christ. We have an organization that is strong and moving forward.

My labor has not been in vain for New Liberty Apostolic Faith Church. We have a church that is strong and growing.

My labor has not been in vain for my family, my children, grandchildren, great-grandchildren, and those yet to be born.

Most of all, my labor has not been in vain for the love of my life, my jewel, my business partner, my home partner, my prayer partner, my best friend, my loving, devoted, committed wife, Mae Dee Boone. She worked beside me, raised the children, kept the books, kept appointments and kept the house. Now that she has come to the real golden years of her life where she can reflect on what God has done, He has given us miracle after miracle. She no longer has to keep the books and write out the bills and drive from place to place. God has given her committed, trustworthy people who keep the books, the house, appointments, and drive her everywhere she wants to go.

I no longer have to work from can see-to-can't see. God has given me faithful, strong armor bearers who have only one question. "Bishop, what do you need?"

It warms my heart and fills my spirit with joy when I see that through my labor and everything I have done, God has brought me to a place where we no longer have to worry about some of the day to day operations of life. God has given me what He gave Moses. Help when I needed it most. *But Moses' hands were heavy; and they took a stone, and put it under him, and he sat thereon; and Aaron and Hur stayed up his hands, the one on the one side, and the other on the other side; and his hands were steady until the going down of the sun. Exodus 17:12*

As I looked out for the lives of God's people, now people are looking out for our lives, my family, my church and the organization.

HOLINESS THE STANDARD OF DRESS

This is my strong conviction.

This is not a reflection on anyone else but me. This is my concept of the scripture. I believe this. I believe all of this. I am not getting out there on some territory I'm not supposed to be on. I don't want nobody calling in and challenging me from what the government and the states are doing, I just want them to know that this is little me, This is my Story. This is what I believe. This is what is in my heart. This is what I practice. This is my interpretation of the scriptures.

This is my Story.

I Will Not
New Liberty Will Not
Apostolic Assemblies of Christ Will Not
Let Down the Standard

*For I am the Lord, I change not...
Malachi 3:6*

If you read that right and look at it right it said it all right there, God does not change.

I am not fighting the designers. Some of the things that they design are good for the world but not good for the church. But if you look at what these designers are doing now they are designing some things that glorify the sinful nature of man and what is detrimental to holiness.

WOMEN - MAINTAINING THE STANDARD OF HOLINESS

But speak thou the things which become sound doctrine...The aged women likewise, that they be in behaviour as becometh holiness, not false accusers, not given to much wine, teachers of good things; That they may teach the young women to be sober, to love their husbands, to love their children, To be discreet, chaste, keepers at home, good, obedient to their own husbands, that the word of God be not blasphemed. Titus 2:1-5

Our churches should have a Mother's Board or something like that in there to give direction, when it comes down to the apparel, because there are some materials and fabrics and styles saints shouldn't even wear. The Mother's Board is the one who should teach the women not to wear dresses that are too short, too tight or too low cut. Some of them dress the way they do because they have not been taught how to dress. If they are built a certain way they should not wear certain things.

The Pastor's wife should be the prime example of the ladies of the church. She, along with the Mother's Board is obligated to teach all women how to dress in a way to honor God.

I've got somebody like that in my church. My daughter-in-law, Rhonda is like that. You sit down with her, she can take this dress thing and make you scratch your head. She's that good. She is very, very, firm with it. She will go point by point, through the doctrine in the scripture, but it is right. *For the Lord taketh pleasure in his people: he will beautify the meek with salvation. Psalm 149:4*

God beautifies the meek with salvation, I think we ought to let God do it. You are saying that you are not pleased or happy with the way God made you when you put on lipstick, cut off eyebrows, make some new ones, wear eye shadow, disarranging your real self and taking away from the beauty that God gave you.

These designers have got you expressing yourself, to yourself and a dying world, saying, "I'm not happy with the way God made me." *A new heart also will I give you, and a new spirit will I put within you: Ezekiel 36:26*

God has taken your heart out and put a new heart in you, and you are still fooling around with the old man.

I'm just going to tell you. I'm against it. I'm real dogmatic and I'm getting more dogmatic. Some of them are waiting. Some of them are hoping that my church is going to go whoop! Off to the left after I pass off the scene and they will be able to let down the standard and start wearing and looking like anything but a Holy Woman of God. The way God put this in me. God is going to stand by me. I feel like nobody is going to be able to bring it down. They are going to run up against a stone wall if anybody tries to go against what God has established in New Liberty Apostolic Faith Church and the Apostolic Assemblies of Christ. God will not allow that to happen. This is the standard that God laid out in His word. This is my conviction.

I am not for putting on all of this decoratorial stuff, other than what God does for you. Even dealing with the wigs, if you have to have one, get one, please cover your head up, but look modest. Modesty still don't mean for you to get a red wig or blonde wig but get one that is age and color appropriate to your natural hair color.

I want to let you know where my heart is. I was responsible for teaching the truth to every member of New Liberty Apostolic Faith Church. As the founder of the Apostolic Assemblies of Christ I was responsible for laying this part of the foundation, before I passed the Mantles. If I did not tell the truth, God was going to hold me responsible. *Cry aloud, spare not, lift up thy voice like a trumpet, and shew my people their transgression, and the house of Jacob their sins. Isaiah 58:1*

MEN AND DRESSING BECOMING TO HOLINESS

I want it to be known that even as far as the men, these old baggy pants and all of this old reflecting it's a lot of things that you see just actually in the spirit of people that I don't like. Men and women with the flirtatious spirit, that is there and I am against that and I think we ought to move away from everything that is not of God that is not pertaining to holiness.

The older men are obligated by the Word of God to do the same thing for the younger men as the women. *But speak thou the things which become sound doctrine: That the aged men be sober, grave, temperate, sound in faith, in charity, in patience. Young men likewise exhort to be sober minded. In all things shewing thyself a pattern of good works: in doctrine shewing uncorruptness, gravity, sincerity, Sound speech, that cannot be condemned; that he that is of the contrary part may be ashamed, having no evil thing to say of you. Titus 2:1-8*

With men, the sagging pants and earrings, all make the statement that you are not honoring God.

I don't mean to knock the fish out of the water, but I want him to know that I troubled his territory.

We've got a story to tell.

I'm named for that. I'm known for that. There is a message to be given in clothing. The principle applies to men also. *And it was told Tamar, saying, Behold thy father in law goeth up to Timnath to shear his sheep. And she put her widow's garments off from her, and covered her with a vail, and wrapped herself, and sat in an open place, which is by the way to Timnath; for she saw that Shelah was grown, and she was not given unto him to wife. When Judah saw her, he thought her to be an harlot; because she had covered her face. And he turned unto her by the way, and said, Go to, I pray thee, let me come in unto thee; (for he knew not that she was his daughter in law.) And she said, What wilt thou give me, that thou mayest come in unto me? And he said, I will send thee a kid from the flock. And she said, Wilt thou give me a pledge, till thou send it? And he said, What pledge shall I give thee? And she said, Thy signet, and thy bracelets, and thy staff that is in thine hand. And he gave it her, and came in unto her, and she conceived by him. Genesis 38:13-18*

MEN AND WOMEN

Exactly as God made us is good enough.

I think basically you coming to my convention, I think my convention looks quite well. You have a few unsaved but you just about know them from the way that they take part in the service. I've had them say they came to the organization because they saw our website. I know a woman in Texas right now, she said when she saw our website, she said those are the women that I want to be a part of when she saw how the women was dressed and all of that. It's just there. It's just a few.

The word that came to Jeremiah from the Lord, saying, Stand in the gate of the Lord's house, and proclaim there this word, and say, Hear the word of the Lord, all ye of Judah, that enter in at these gates to worship the Lord. Thus saith the Lord of hosts, the God of Israel, Amend your ways and your doings, and I will cause you to dwell in this place. Jeremiah 7:1-3

It's just like the Lord told Jeremiah to stand in the gates of the house of the Lord to proclaim to Israel old path and finally walk therein, they deliberately said we will not, he told them if you do it I will bless you. They refused, were captured and carried into the land of Babylon.

You don't need a lot of people to make it happen. But those of us who are here must establish and maintain the excellence of the standard that God laid out for us. God meant what He said.

Holiness is not just talking it, it is living it and looking it also, God's requirement is a body of believers looking like they are saved.

Proper attire is just another way of identifying us as lights of the world, or "saints of God." It is important that our identification not be counterfeit. We should clearly reflect the image of Christ. *What? know ye not that your body is the temple of the Holy Ghost which is in you, which ye have of God, and ye are not your own?*
I Corinthians 6:19

Let us know that our bodies are the temples of the living God. It is such an honor for God to dwell within us. So, we should be very careful how we adorn the temple of God. Since we are ambassadors for Christ, *Now then we are ambassadors for Christ, as though God did beseech you by us: we pray you in Christ's stead, be ye reconciled to God. II Corinthians 5:20*

Whose adorning let it not be that outward adorning of plaiting the hair, and of wearing of gold, or of putting on of apparel; But let it be the hidden man of the heart, in that which is not corruptible, even the ornament of a meek and quiet spirit, which is in the sight of God of great price. I Peter 3:3-4

We should not use clothing for vainglory, props, or show offs. *Let nothing be done through strife or vainglory; but in lowliness of mind let each esteem other better than themselves. Philippians 2:3*

Remember the style of clothing you select reflects who you really are. It has been said, *...for the Lord seeth not as man seeth; for man looketh on the* *outward appearance, but the Lord looketh on the heart. I Samuel 16:7*

Yes, God judges the heart of man, but what is in your heart should not send conflicting signals of what the outward person is signifying. For example, your profession should be easily identified, as a police officer is recognized by a uniform, a construction worker by hard hats and steel toe shoes, or a street woman by her seductive and loose, revealing clothing. So you see, proper clothing identifies who you represent. I want to let you know where my heart is.

For it is better, if the will of God be so, that ye suffer for well doing, than for evil doing. Which sometime were disobedient, when once the longsuffering of God waited in the days of Noah, while the ark was a preparing, wherein few, that is, eight souls were saved by water. I Peter 3:17, 20

It's just a few like in the days of Noah, if you've got 1/8 of the people now looking to the altar for holiness, you are doing well. But those of us who know the way must teach the way correctly and let our example show the world who and what we are.

This is what my church is, and my church and organization teaches against anything that is against holiness.

I want the world to see holiness exemplified.

I want those who are coming behind me to see that it is not what it used to be it is what it is now. Not as far as people getting up testifying, well you used to couldn't do this. You used to couldn't do that. Pertaining to well you couldn't go to the movies, you couldn't do this. You couldn't do that. It is all still good.

About the dress code, holiness is not just talking it, it is living it and looking it also, God's requirement is a body of believers looking like they are saved.

I want this clear to let them know that I am not putting anybody out but nobody at my church is going to be up in my choir, in my auxiliaries, ushering or doing anything with all this stuff on. That is a no-no. I don't intend to accept it. I won't accept it. We don't have to do it. But they will remain as laity in the church and not in a leadership role until they come up to the standards laid down by God in His word and upheld by New Liberty and the Apostolic Assemblies of Christ. Before I even put them up to do anything, I want it clear that they must come up to the standard. It will not happen otherwise.

One thing I believe that God can beautify you better than anybody else.

We just don't do it.

And modesty in apparel.

I'm really hung on that and I'll never take down on it.

I leave you with the reminder and confirmation from God's word that how God made men and women is good enough. *I will praise thee; for I am fearfully and wonderfully made: marvellous are thy works; and that my soul knoweth right well. Psalm 139:14*

With all of these things, I feel like now that I have told about the farm, family, army, wife, children, preaching, pastoring, founding a church and an organization, I can say, I am completely in the Will of God.

I can now say, This Is My Story.

I want you to pray for me, I'm thanking God for these over 50 years of pastoral service, and over 90 years and how God started and brought me up through the ranks from five years old to 95 years of age and I am a happy man today. And I believe God has a charge for my ministry and we thank God for what He has done for us.

God bless you.

As the summary of this great man's life comes to bear,
we can think of him as he faced his careful and challenging childhood,
his tough and tireless teens;
his thoughtful and technical twenties;
his thankful and toiling thirties,
his favorable and forgiving forties;
his fearless and faithful fifties;
his seasonal and sensational sixties;
his sensible and scholastic seventies;
his earnest and effective eighties;
his noble and neighborly nineties
and look with great anticipation toward his happy, hallowed and hallelujah
hundred.

HEAVEN IS WAITING FOR YOU THROUGH THE GRAVE OR THROUGH THE RAPTURE AND I EXPECT TO SEE YOU THERE, IN THAT GREAT GETTING UP MORNING WHEN THE SOULS OF JUST MEN ARE ALL MADE PERFECT.

Yours Because Of Calvary,
Dr. Lovora J. Walker

Congratulations
BISHOP BOONE

THE WHITE HOUSE
WASHINGTON

from
BARACK H. OBAMA
44th President of the United States

STATE OF MICHIGAN
EXECUTIVE OFFICE
LANSING

RICK SNYDER
GOVERNOR

BRIAN CALLEY
LT. GOVERNOR

July 10, 2015

Dear Bishop G.M. Boone:

I hope this letter finds you well on the momentous celebration of your 95th birthday. I am honored to acknowledge this joyous milestone filled with memories and experiences. It is not only a time of happiness, but a time to reflect on the lives you have enriched. Michigan has been truly fortunate to share in your long legacy of achievement.

I join with your family, friends and the entire state in congratulating you on this special occasion.

Sincerely,

Rick Snyder
Governor

GEORGE W. ROMNEY BUILDING • 111 SOUTH CAPITOL AVENUE • LANSING, MICHIGAN 48909
www.michigan.gov

CITY OF DETROIT

Certificate of
RECOGNITION

Founder of the New Liberty Apostolic Faith Church in Detroit, Bishop George Marshall Boone is known, both nationally and internationally, for his relentless efforts in the ministry. With over 50 years in the pastoral ministry, Bishop Boone is also founder of the Apostolic Assemblies of Christ.

A true community servant, Bishop Boone holds summer camp each year for youth, organizes a backpack rally for back to school supplies, provides a food pantry to feed the hungry and serves healthy meals during the summer. Through these various acts of kindness, Bishop Boone shows his dedication, love and compassion for others.

Therefore, I, Mike Duggan, Mayor of the city of Detroit, do hereby congratulate

BISHOP GEORGE MARSHALL BOONE

on the occasion of his 95th Birthday

Your life is a living testament that God provides and protects his faithful servants.

_____
Mayor, City of Detroit

JULY 10, 2015
_____
Date

PENTECOSTAL ASSEMBLIES OF THE WORLD, INC
OFFICE OF THE PRESIDER - BISHOP CHARLES H. ELLIS III
(EPISCOPAL OFFICE)
P.O. BOX 21909RATS
DETROIT, MICHIGAN 48221
313-543-6063   313-543-6067 (FAX)

JULY 2015

A MESSAGE OF CONGRATULATIONS
TO
BISHOP GEORGE M. BOONE

MY WIFE CRISETTE AND I AND ALL THAT WE REPRESENT PAUSE TO SALUTE YOU ON CELEBRATING 95 YEARS OF LIFE. AS MY DAD WOULD SAY, *"DOWN THROUGH THE YEARS GOD HAS TRULY BEEN GOOD TO YOU."* YOU HAVE TRULY BECOME ONE OF OUR EXEMPLARY APOSTOLIC FATHERS AND YOUR INTEGRITY AND LOVE FOR GOD SPEAKS TO HIS BLESSINGS UPON YOU THESE MANY YEARS.

I REMAIN IN AWE ON HOW THE LORD HAS STRENGTHENED YOU TO ESTABLISH THE NEW LIBERTY APOSTOLIC FAITH CHURCH AS WELL AS THE APOSTOLIC ASSEMBLIES OF CHRIST WHICH TOGETHER HAVE LAUNCHED MANY OTHER MINISTRIES AND KINGDOM WORKS. I HAVE LONG ADMIRED YOU AND CONSIDERED YOUR FAMILY TO BE MY FAMILY. I WILL FOREVER CHERISH THE FELLOWSHIP AND KINDNESS THAT YOU AND MOTHER MAE DEE HAVE EXTENDED TO ME OVER THE YEARS.

IT IS MY PRAYER THAT YOU WILL GREATLY ENJOY YOUR TIME OF FESTIVITIES AND MAY THE LORD CONTINUE TO BRING TO PASS EVERY WORD YOU SPEAK... WE LOVE YOU TO LIFE!

CWH Ellis III

PRESIDING BISHOP

Pentecostal Churches
of the Apostolic Faith, Assn., International
"Empowered by the Holy Spirit, we are touching the world with the life-transforming message of Jesus Christ"

Bishop J E Moore
Presiding Prelate of the Pentecostal Churches of the Apostolic Faith, Int.
723 South 45th Street
Louisville, Kentucky 40211

To the Honorable Bishop G. M. Boone, D.D., the founder of The Apostolic Assemblies of Christ, Inc.

I would like to express my heartfelt congratulations on the publishing of your book, "This Is My Story". I am delighted to see your work come to fruition, many have attempted to start extensive undertakings, but you have accomplished and surpassed those by building and establishing a phenomenal, and flourishing organization, the (AAofC).

I am sure that this book will be overflowing with the wisdom, knowledge and insight from an anointed vessel of God who has an illustrious and impressive life and walk with the Lord.

The most exciting and prolific novels written are those that focus on real life, trials, struggles and triumphs.

I am sure that your book will be an instrument for inspiring many who may travel the paths that you have lead by example and I believe that we will benefit from the years of life of this insightful biblical scholar.

You are a distinguished and celebrated Man of God with a legacy lived to be proclaimed to all, who has taken his time and gifts to invite humanity into his life and exemplify the story of your life.

May the Lord God bless the sale of this book that it would reach the hands and hearts of many and may they find comfort for the toils of life and encouragement to go forward in ministry.

God Bless You

Bishop J E Moore

Presiding Prelate, Bishop J E Moore

Apostolic World Christian Fellowship, Inc.

Officers

Bishop Samuel Smith, General Chairman
    Evansville, Indiana
Bishop David Fuller, Vice Chairman
    Waco, Texas
Bishop Clarence Haddon, 2nd Vice Chairman
    Detroit, Michigan
Bishop Wayne Green, General Secretary
    Upper Marlboro, Maryland
Pastor Reynaldo Leal, General Treasurer
    Bell Gardens, California
Bishop A. L. Henderson, Ambassador-at-Large
    Bremen, Georgia
Bishop Ralph E. Green, Honorary
Bishop David Rowe, Honorary

Executive Committee

Bishop D. Rayford Bell, Chairman
    Evanston, Illinois
Bishop Samuel Smith
    Evansville, Indiana
Bishop David Fuller
    Waco, Texas
Bishop Clarence Haddon
    Detroit, Michigan
Reverend Billy Shoulders
    Nashville, Tennessee
Bishop P.D. Rowe
    Mishawaka, Indiana
Bishop Alphonso Scott
    St. Louis, Missouri

June 9, 2015

Greetings in the all-powerful name of our Lord Jesus Christ. I pray that this letter finds you all well and blessed.

I am privileged to convey my expressions of appreciation for, and congratulations to, the honorable Bishop G.M. Boone, D.D., on this very special occasion of his 9545 Celebration.

Bishop Boone is a living legend among amongst Apostolics everywhere. It has been my distinct honor to have known him over the years. His presence at our AWCF World Congresses was always a blessing. His wisdom and integrity has always been admired by all who were blessed to be in his fellowship.

On behalf of the entire AWCF membership worldwide, we wish Bishop Boone a wonderful 9545 Celebration. We pledge our prayers for his continued health and ministry.

In Christ,

Bishop Samuel Smith
General Chairman
Apostolic World Christian Fellowship

P.O. Box 3924 • Evansville, Indiana 47737 USA
Office (812) 464-1175 • Fax (812) 468-8235 • Web site: www.awcf.org • E-mail: awcf@sigecom.net

108 THIS IS MY STORY

*... I continue
unto this day ...*

~ **Acts 26:22**

BISHOP G.M. BOONE, D.D. **109**

MY PARENTS' MARRIAGE CERTIFICATE

STATE OF MISSISSIPPI

Certificate of Marriage

LAFAYETTE COUNTY

I, Mrs. Verna McElreath, Clerk of the Circuit Court of said County and State and Custodian of the Marriage Records thereof, do hereby certify that the said Marriage Records show that on the ___25___ day of ___March___ 19_15_

The Rites of Matrimony
were celebrated between

Book _U_

Page No. _48_

Mr. _S. Boone_ and

M _Felder Coleman_

By _F. L. Coleman_

M. G.

Given under my hand and Seal of said Court, this _8th_ day of _January_ 19_58_

Mrs. Verna S. McElreath Circuit Clerk

D. C.

My Parents

*I got along very, very well with my mama and daddy.
It was a lovely relationship. Both of them were jewels.
My mother loved me. My daddy loved me.
They both were School teachers.
They treated me very well.*

My Parents, My Siblings, Nieces and Nephews

Sometimes we thought the discipline and what they said didn't make sense and sometimes they jacked you up but in the end, I guess it worked. I had 12 sisters; I was right in the middle with six beneath and six above. As I came on up with my older sisters, the six that were above me I was familiar with them and of course the younger siblings came later and as every one of them came in I accepted them graciously as part of the family.

MY FATHER

My father, Shepherd Boone graduated from High School in 1887 from Mississippi State Normal School in Holly Springs, Mississippi.

The Annual Commencement was held at The Masonis Hall on May 26, 1887.

He understood the importance of education and pursued it relentlessly with the support of his father. During the 1800's it was very tough for a negro (as people of African descent was referred to) to achieve education due to the circumstances surrounding them. Many of them had no transportation and schools were miles away, and many children had to maintain farming duties to support their families.

Discrimination against a person of color was a very big part of it. The negro's found it hard to gain admissions into higher institutions. Consequently, most Negros had a farm, perform handy works or work as sharecroppers.

Daddy continued his quest in educating himself while taking care of his family in The Making of The Boone Clan.

On August 18, 1944, my father received his Teacher Certificate from the State of Mississippi. It is important to note that he retired from teaching the same school year.

In order for him to earn his teacher's certificate, he not only had to complete the course requirements but he also had to complete a required amount of classroom teaching hours to earn his certificate.

A school year back in those days, went from the month of October thru the month of March. This allowed the children of farmers the time they needed for the months of harvesting, to be able to work in the field. During the summer months, my father also taught school on a college level at Rust College in Holly Springs, Mississippi. This gave him the opportunity to earn extra money for his household. He taught school for 25 to 30 years.

My father died of a heart attack on September 27, 1957. He was 89 years old.

MY MOTHER

My mother lived to be 79 years old before she made her transition. In her living years, she was a compassionate mother and devout Christian. She adhered to the upbringing of her parents and instilled within her children a love for God, good common sense, education, and strong moral values.

Mother must have had insight of the tragedies that strike so many families at the time of loss of a parent and did not want her children to suffer that devastation. Because, while on her deathbed, she continued to instill obedience to her children, and her words were put into action through her children. Those words still ring out of the mouths of young and old Boones alike. That simple command made by Mama to her children was, "Stick Together".

My mother died on February 6, 1970.

My niece Eleanor McChriston, put the power of Mama's words into action by writing a song for the Boone Clan entitled "God Bless Our Family". Since the writing of the song, the Boones have adopted it as their theme song. It is sang at every family reunion. Here is the family song:

God bless our family, let love shine around,
Keep us loving and caring, as your loving grace abounds.
May we share all of life's blessings
To our offspring, as best we can

CHORUS: God bless our family,
The Boones of today,
God bless our family,
In your name we pray.

Grand-ma Fielda told us, together stay as one.

"Stick together", forever; and that is our intention.

Love each other; sisters and brothers, Aunts and uncles, and cousins, too!!!

LETTER FROM MY FATHER

Route 1 Box 146
Oxford Miss
March 17, 1952

Dear Son & Family

I received your most welcome letter a few days ago and I appreciate your advice to the highest. Yes we all are well doing nicely. Hope the same of you all. Hope that O.K. Well continue to be your Oh yes I've finished cleaning my new ground and has the wood on the yard and if I am thinking of getting some of the boys to break it for me. Should I undertake it? I am expecting to be more careful but I feel that its my lot to stay on the move. Hope success will continue on well with you.

Give my regards to all.

I remain your Father
Shepherd Boone

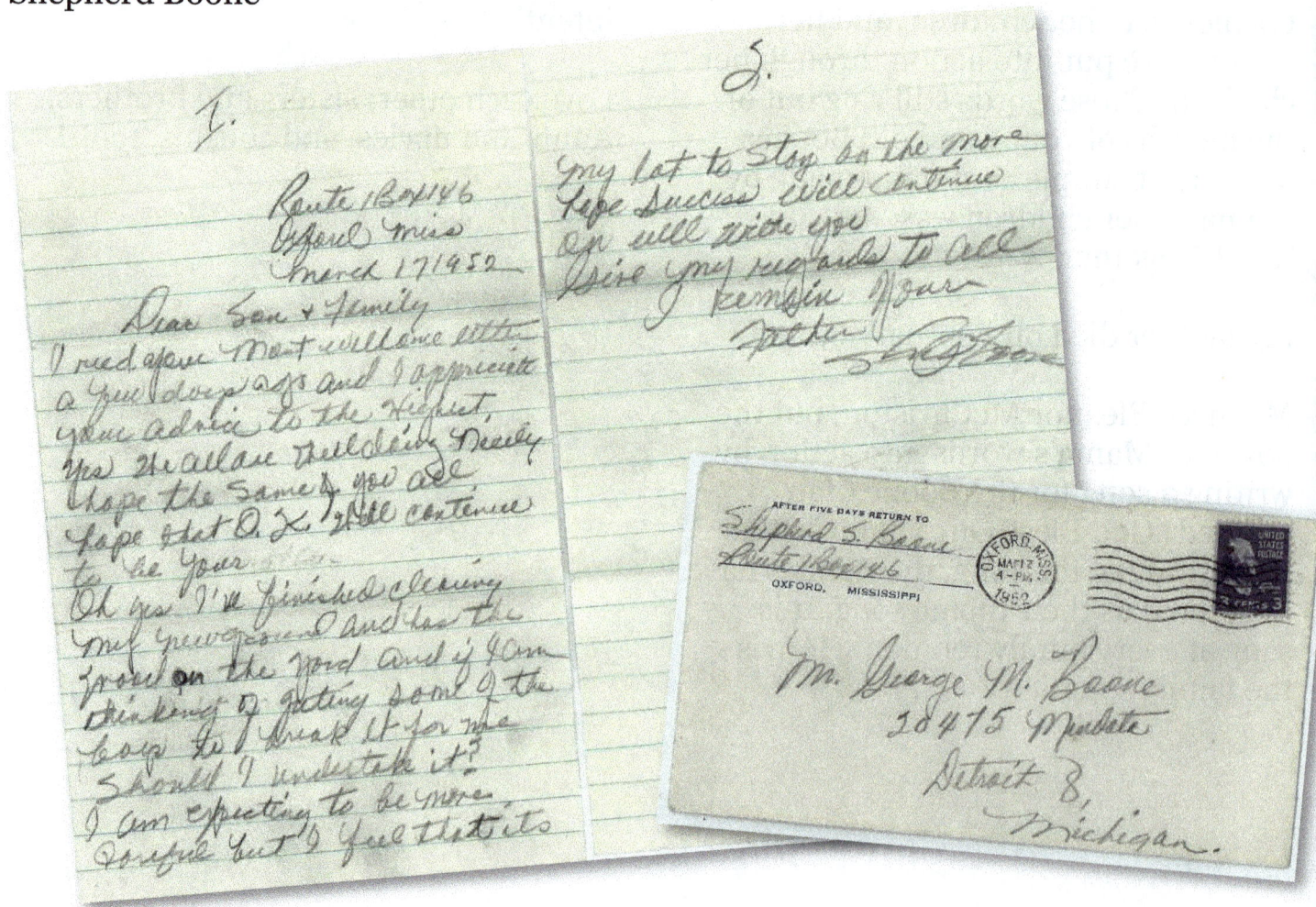

LETTER FROM MY MOTHER

Oxford Miss
November 9, 1957

Dear Son

I rec'd your letter and money and I thank you very much. At present all are doing very well. The Dr. said I was doing fine. He gave me a good exam and then an x-ray an electrocardiograph. He told me to come back in three or four months. I guess if I keep doing well I will be dismissed. Easter and Tom has been picking cotton for Rev. Lockhart. He has two or three more days picking. I guess Easter will help him thru when the weather gets dry enough. We have had some very cool weather and two big frosts. Now it is raining. I am looking for a $10 load of fire and stove wood today. Has Dott ever found a job? She wrote once and said she had quit her job because it was too hard.

I think Zone and James has done so wonderful. They sent $25 at one time and then sent $70.00 $29.00 to go on the funeral and the rest for me. Mr. Caruthers is still on the sick list. He does'nt seem to get much better. Tender my regards to Mae Dee and all the rest of my girls. I haven't heard from Myrtle in a long time. Now son you must remember the house can't last long with the high cost of living and wood and other household expenses. I haven't had an offer on the land yet. I am waiting for someone to come. I am not acting over anxious. Well I guess this is all.

Yours Lovingly
Mother

MY GRANDPARENTS

Nancy Boone

Moses Boone

Marshall Coleman

Millie Coleman

I Knew my Grandparents

My Mother and My Sisters

I have such vivid memories of spending quality time with my sisters in Memphis. After my sister Dorothy, who we all affectionately called "Dot" and her husband Donald relocated from Chicago to Memphis, Dot's house became a gathering place for my sisters and I. Because of the strong love that our family possesses, we would sometimes sit around the table eating, laughing and enjoying each other's company while reflecting on times past.

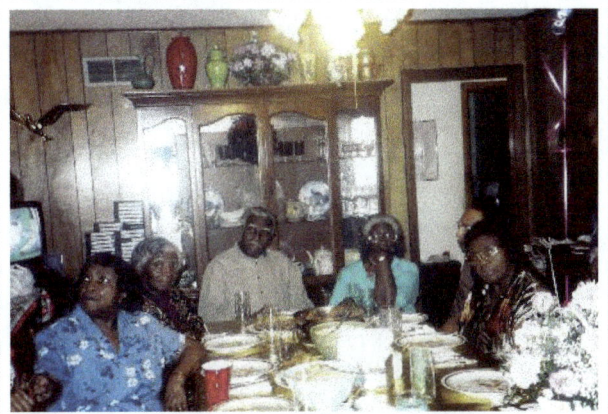

Thanks for the Memories

BISHOP G.M. BOONE, D.D. **121**

SERMONS BY BISHOP G.M. BOONE

1964-1965

1964

Date: September 6, 1964
Scripture: Luke 15:11-15
Sermon Title: Wasted Goods in a Far Country

Date: September 13, 1964
Scriptures: I Corinthians 15; Isaiah 6:1
Sermon Title: In the Year King Uzziah Died, I Saw the Lord

Date: September 20, 1964
Scriptures: Acts 9:15-17; Psalms 57:7
Sermon Title: Who Shall Separate Us? - "A Fixed Heart"

Date: September 27, 1964
Scriptures: I Timothy 4:14; Psalms 19:14
Sermon Title: Get Right, Be Right and Stay Right

Date: October 4, 1964
Scriptures: Isaiah 46:8; Isaiah 45:22
Sermon Title: Look ye unto me – all the ends of the earth

Date: October 18, 1964
Scripture: Acts 16:24-28
Sermon Title: One Way Out

Date: October 25, 1964
Scripture: Isaiah 35:8
Sermon Title: The Highway of Holiness

Date: November 1, 1964
Scriptures: Ezekiel 22:27-30; Jeremiah 5:1-2
Sermon Title: God Wants a Man - "Evil Times"

Date: November 8, 1964
Scripture: Exodus
Sermon Title: God's Purpose in Us

Date: November 15, 1964
Scriptures: Lamentations 3:19-23; 3:1
Sermon Title: God's Mercies

Date: November 29, 1964
Scripture: Ephesians 4
Sermon Title: God's Purpose in Us and for Us

1965

Date: January 3, 1965
Scripture: St. John 16:32-33
Sermon Title: Be of Good Cheer in this World of Tribulation

Date: January 10, 1965
Scripture: Exodus 15:1-5
Sermon Title: God is a Man of War and the Lord is his Name

Date: January 17, 1965
Scriptures: Isaiah 51:1-4; Hebrews 3:7
Sermon Title: Hearken Unto Me

Date: January 31, 1965
Scriptures: II Thessalonians 1:3-7; Job 3:17
Sermon Title: Joys of the Future Life

Date: February 7, 1965
Scriptures: Nehemiah 2:19-20; Psalms 1:3
Sermon Title: The God of Heaven, He will Prosper us, Therefore We will Rise and Build

Date: February 14, 1965
Scripture:
Sermon Title: Judgment Message Given to the Saints

Date: February 21, 1965
Scriptures: Luke 13:1-3; Mark 1:15
Sermon Title: Repent Ye and Believe the Gospel

Date: February 28, 1965
Scripture: Jude 1:1-4
Sermon Title: Earnestly Contend for the Faith

Date: March 14, 1965
Scriptures: Acts 4:16; Mark 10:21
Sermon Title: Holiness is Right; We Cannot Deny it

Date: April 4, 1965
Scripture: Psalms 34:17
Sermon Title: Everything is All Right

Date: April 11, 1965
Scripture: Jeremiah 10:19-24
Sermon Title: Correct Me, but Not in Judgment

Date: April 18, 1965
Scriptures: Matthew 28:6-8; I Peter 1:3
Sermon Title: A Lively Hope by His Resurrection

Date: April 25, 1965
Scripture: Philippians 1:17
Sermon Title: Set for the Defense of the Gospel

Date: May 2, 1965
Scriptures: II Chronicles 15:1-4; Matthew 28:19-20
Sermon Title: Lo I am with You so Observe All Things

Date: May 9, 1965
Scripture: Matthew 12:46-49
Sermon Title: Behold My Mother: An Ideal Mother

Date: May 16, 1965
Scripture: Job 23:8-12
Sermon Title: Confidence

Date: May 27, 1965
Scripture: St. John 4:35
Sermon Title: Zeal for Souls

Date: May 30, 1965
Scripture: Psalms 16:8
Sermon Title: I shall not be moved

Date: June 6, 1965
Scriptures: James 1:13-15; Jeremiah 7:3
Sermon Title: Amend Your Ways

Date: June 13, 1965
Scriptures: I Timothy 4:8; Isaiah 3:10
Sermon Title: Godliness is Profitable

Date: June 27, 1965
Scriptures: Jeremiah 18:1-6; St. John 3:6
Sermon Title: A New Vessel

Date: July 4, 1965
Scriptures: Matthew 4:17; Luke 14:26-30
Sermon Title: Failure

Date: July 11, 1965
Scriptures: Proverbs 24:10; I Corinthians 4:8-10
Sermon Title: A Day of Adversity

Date: July 18, 1965
Scriptures: Proverbs 4:23; Acts 2:40-42
Sermon Title: Save Yourself

Date: July 25, 1965
Scripture: Psalms 119:165
Sermon Title: Great Peace Have They who Love thy Law and Nothing Shall Offend Them

Date: August 9, 1965
Scriptures: Genesis 2:16-17; Isaiah 57:15
Sermon Title: Trouble! Trouble! God Will Revive the Contrite Heart

Date: August 10, 1965
Scripture: Genesis 35:1-5
Sermon Title: Be Clean and Change Your Garments

Date: August 13, 1965
Scripture: Matthew 16:24
Sermon Title: Self Denial

Date: August 29, 1965
Scriptures: Jeremiah 31; Romans 5:7
Sermon Title: God's Sacrificial Love

Date: September 5, 1965
Scriptures: II Corinthians 5:10; Hebrews 10:30-31
Sermon Title: It is a Fearful Thing to fall into the Hands of a Living God

Date: September 12, 1965
Scripture: I Peter 4:17-19
Sermon Title: Testing Time

SOME OF MY FAVORITE SONGS

JUST OVER IN THE GLORY LAND
NO NOT ONE
BE DONE
ONE MORE TIME
FOOTPRINTS OF JESUS
WON'T IT BE GRAND
ROCK OF AGES
IS YOUR ALL ON THE ALTAR
I'LL FLY AWAY
BECAUSE HE LOVED ME SO
I LOVE HIM
NEAR THE CROSS
SWEET SPIRIT
O SOUL AWAKE
PUT YOUR TIME IN
CHRIST IS ALL
UNDER THE BLOOD
ON MY WAY TO HEAVEN
FATHER, I STRETCH MY HANDS TO THEE
'TIS SO SWEET TO TRUST IN JESUS

BISHOP BOONE'S BOOK & BOOKLETS

Book
1.) Now that you're Saved "Sanctify yourself and be ye Holy"

Several booklets:
1.) "Effective Ministries: Pastors and Associate Ministers working together for Kingdom building"

2.) "A Cohesive Ministry"

3.) "God's Plan for the Family"

4.) "A Polished Minister"

5.) "Pastor's Protocol and Parliamentary Procedures"

6.) "Unified Pastors with a Unified Vision"

7.) "Partners in Progress: Pastors/Ministers and their Companions working together in Harmony"

BISHOP BOONE HAS TOUCHED THE WORLD

For 45 years the Apostolic Assemblies of Christ has had 32 States and 6 Countries

Alabama • Arkansas • Arizona • California • Colorado • Florida • Georgia
Hawaii • Illinois • Indiana • Iowa • Kansas • Kentucky • Louisiana
Maryland • Massachusetts • Michigan • Mississippi • Missouri • Nebraska
North Carolina • Ohio • Oklahoma • South Carolina • Tennessee • Texas
Utah • Virginia • Washington • West Virginia • Wisconsin • Wyoming

Liberia • Germany • Guam • Haiti • Japan • New Guinea

BISHOP'S FAMOUS SAYINGS

"Go way from here"

"I am a three quarter tosh"

"I got marble & chalk, duce & a quarter & I don't have to walk"

"I got marble & chalk, Cadillac 8 & I don't have to walk"

"Tell me what you're gonna do, business is calling, ain't got time to monk around"

"Partner"

"Bite the bullet & keep on stepping"

"We gonna Rock Daniel"

"Sha"

"Let the good time roll"

"If you don't stand for something, you will fall for anything"

"This will eat right where you hold it"

"Don't start nothing & it won't be nothing"

"Let's eat"

"Holy God"

"To know me is to love me"

"Cracking the whip"

"I'll put your back on the ground"

"Roll with the punches"

"Let's have it"

"Loose here"

"What's on log for lizard"

"Is that right"

"Keep your head above the water"

"Rise Peter slay and eat"

BISHOP'S FAVORITES

Favorite **SEASON**: Spring & Fall

Favorite **SCRIPTURES**:

"Having therefore obtained help of God, I continue unto this day . . ." Acts 26:22

"Stand fast therefore in the liberty wherewith Christ hath made us free, and be not entangled again with the yoke of bondage." Galatians 5:1

Favorite **BIBLE**: Thompson Chain

Favorite **HOBBY**: Riding Horses, Planting Flowers & Working in his Garden

Favorite **HORSE**: Tennessee Walker

Favorite **COLOR of HORSE**: Black & Chestnut

Favorite type of **CAR**: Lexus

Favorite **STATE**: Mississippi

Favorite way to **TRAVEL**: Car

Favorite **FOODS**: Soul Food

Favorite **DESSERTS**: Banana Pudding & 3-layer cake with Chocolate Icing

Favorite **MEATS**: Chicken & Fish

Favorite **WILD GAME**: Rabbit

Favorite **HOT BEVERAGE**: Coffee

Favorite **COLD POP**: Root Beer

Favorite **HOLIDAY**: Thanksgiving

Favorite **MUSIC**: Good Quartet

Favorite **INSTRUMENT**: Lead Guitar

Favorite **SONGS**: "Just Over In The Glory Land" & "No Not One"

Favorite **WATCH**: Rolex

95 THINGS ABOUT BISHOP BOONE

1. ADMIRED
2. ANOINTED
3. APOSTOLIC
4. APPOINTED
5. APPRECIATED
6. AUTHOR
7. BELOVED
8. BISHOP
9. BLESSED
10. BUILDER
11. CARING
12. CHARISMA
13. CONCERN
14. CONFIDENTIAL
15. CONSECRATED
16. COUNSELOR
17. COURAGEOUS
18. DEDICATED
19. DEVOTED
20. DISTINGUISHED
21. DYNAMIC
22. EFFECTIVE
23. ENERGETIC
24. EVANGELIST
25. EXCITING
26. FATHER
27. FAITHFUL
28. FOUNDER

29. FRIENDLY
30. GENTLEMEN
31. GIFTED
32. GIVER
33. GODLY
34. GRANDFATHER
35. HAPPY
36. HISTORIAN
37. HOLY
38. HONEST

39. HOSPITABLE
40. HUMBLE
41. HUSBAND
42. INSPIRING
43. INTREGATIVE
44. INTELLIGENT
45. JOYFUL
46. JUBILANT
47. JUST
48. KEEN

49. KIND
50. KNOWLEDGABLE
51. LEADER
52. LEGEND
53. LOVING
54. LOYAL
55. MEEK
56. MENTOR
57. MERCIFUL
58. MESSENGER

59. MINISTER
60. MORALLY CLEAN
61. MOTIVATOR
62. NEAT
63. NOBLE
64. OVERSEER
65. PASTOR
66. PEOPLE PERSON
67. PIONEER
68. PRAISER

69. PREACHER
70. PRESIDING
    BISHOP
71. PROMOTER
72. PROVIDER
73. QUICK
74. RELIABLE
75. RESOURCEFUL
76. RIGHTEOUS
77. SANCTIFIED
78. SERVANT
79. SHEPHERD
80. SINCERE
81. SOLIDER
82. SPIRITUAL
83. STRONG
84. TEACHER
85. TRAINER
86. TRUSTWORTHY
87. UNDERSTANDING
88. UPRIGHT
89. VICTORIOUS
90. VITAL
91. WARRIOR
92. WORTHY
93. YOUTHFUL
94. X-CELLENT
95. ZEALOUS

LOOK AT GOD...
AT 95 YEARS OLD I AM STILL...

Married to my one and only wife 69 years
Counseling * Teaching * Riding Horses

Planting Flowers
Working in my Garden
Traveling * Exciting
Walking * Cooking * Driving

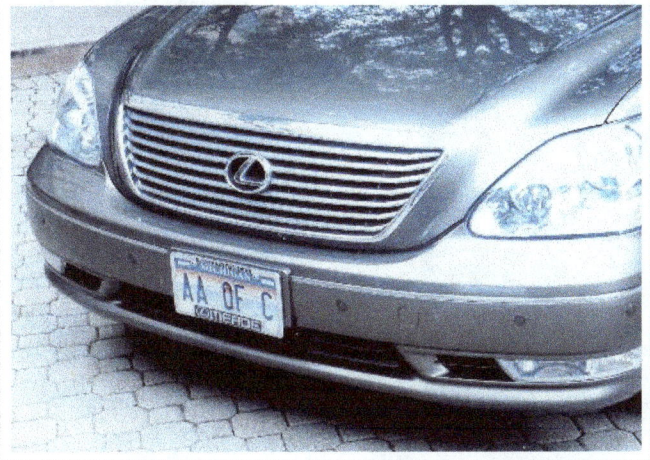

Good Memory * Shouting
Eating Good
Enjoying Jesus and Life

The Lord will preserve him, and keep him alive; and he shall be blessed upon the earth... Psalm 41:2

I AM AFFECTIONATELY CALLED

George • Daddy • Dad • Bishop • Granddaddy • Doc • Tush
Good Daddy • Good Doc • Brother • Uncle George
Brother George • Pastor • Founder • Presiding Bishop
My Bishop • My Pastor • Chief • Grand Bishop
Reverend Boone • General • Boss

YEAR OF 2015 HIGHLIGHTS

for
THE HONORABLE BISHOP
G.M. BOONE, D.D.

95th
NATURAL BIRTHDAY

71st
SPIRITUAL BIRTHDAY

69
YEARS OF MARRIAGE

66
YEARS IN THE MINISTRY

51
YEARS FOUNDER
of theNew Liberty
Apostolic Faith Church
of the Apostolic Assemblies of Christ, Inc.
Detroit, Michigan

45
YEARS FOUNDER
of the Apostolic Assemblies of Christ, Inc.

BISHOP LIVE ON THE WORD NETWORK

HIGHLIGHTS OF
THE HONORABLE
BISHOP G.M. BOONE, D.D.

"A Pioneer, A Legend of his time"

1944

Received the precious gift of the Holy Ghost
in the Jungles of New Guinea

1946

Baptized in the Name of Jesus in Oxford, Mississippi by
District Elder Rush L. Lockhart, Sr.
Married Sister Mae Dee Lockhart

1947-1959

Father of: George Ralph, GeRonald, Charles David, Alfred Heardie, Sharon Ann &
Shirley Ann

1949

Accepted the call to the Ministry

1953

Asst. Pastor of the Zion Apostolic Faith Church - Ferndale, Michigan
Bishop Heardie Leaston, Pastor

1958

Chairman - Michigan State Council of the Pentecostal Churches of the Apostolic
Faith (PCAF)

1961

Ordained Elder by Bishop S.N. Hancock

1962

District Elder

1964

Founded the New Liberty Apostolic Faith Church - Detroit, Michigan
with (23) chartered members

1965
Elevated to the office of Bishop

1970
Founded the Apostolic Assemblies of Christ, Inc. with (7) churches

1970 - Present
Building the Apostolic Assemblies of Christ, Inc.

1989
Received his Doctor of Divinity, Doctor of Ministries, Doctor of Theology from the School of the Apostolic Academy of Christ, Cincinnati, Ohio

1992
Received his Doctor of Philosophy from the School of the Apostolic Academy of Christ, Cincinnati, Ohio

1996
1st live recording of the: Apostolic Assemblies of Christ, Inc.
Featured Songs: "No Not One" & "Christ Is All"

2012
Honored & Received the Apostolic Torch from the Apostolic World Christian Fellowship for the longest served Presiding Bishop in the Apostolic Movement

Passed the Mantle to Bishop Donald Sorrells, D.D. as Presiding Bishop of the Apostolic Assemblies of Christ, Inc.

2015

Passed the Mantle to District Elder J.O. Rasul as Pastor
of the New Liberty Apostolic Faith Church of the
Apostolic Assemblies of Christ, Inc.

Apostolic Assemblies of Christ, Inc.

Alabama, Arkansas, California, Florida, Georgia, Illinois, Indiana, Kentucky,
Louisiana, Maryland, Massachusetts, Michigan, Mississippi, North Carolina, Ohio,
South Carolina, Tennessee, Texas

Countries: Haiti & Africa (9) Councils (7) National Auxiliaries (21) Bishops (5)
Jurisdictional Bishops (16) District Elders

THANKFUL FOR THE ARMY

I began to think about how the Lord Himself how that He embraced me and supported me through the struggle of life being one of the young black men that was raised up in the south,
down in the State of Mississippi, where it was known as one of the most prejudiced states in the nation.

And I think about how that the Lord has carried me all through my army life, the hard things I experienced in my army life, seeing so many thousands of men killed and brought to destruction by the great machine guns and bombs and what have you.
I say but the Lord spared my life and that makes me very thankful today. I thank Him for it today.

UNITED STATES OF AMERICA

Certification of
Military Service

****

This certifies that	George M. Boone 34 486 876
was a member of the	Army of the United States
from	December 7, 1942
to	January 12, 1946
Service was terminated by	Honorable Discharge
Last Grade, Rank, or Rating	Private First Class
Active Service Dates	Same As Above

Date of Birth: Not Available   Place of Birth: Not Available

****

Given at St. Louis, Missouri on November 12, 2010

National Personnel Records Center
(Military Personnel Records)
National Archives and Records Administration

THE ARCHIVIST OF THE UNITED STATES IS THE PHYSICAL CUSTODIAN OF THIS PERSON'S MILITARY RECORD

This Certification of Military Service is issued in the absence of a copy of the actual Report of Separation or its equivalent. This document serves as verification of military service and may be used for any official purpose. Not valid without official seal.

NATIONAL ARCHIVES AND RECORDS ADMINISTRATION   NA FORM 13038 (REV. 04-01)

National Personnel Records Center

Military Personnel Records, *9700 Page Avenue St. Louis, Missouri 63132-5100*

November 15, 2010

GEORGE BOONE
C/O SHEILA PERRY, JFHQ-ILANG
1301 N MACARTHUR BLVD
SPRINGFIELD, IL 62702

> **RE:** **Veteran's Name:** BOONE, George Marshall
> **SSN/SN:** ******396
> **Request Number:** 1-7588066467

Dear Sir:

The record needed to answer your inquiry is not in our files. If the record were here on July 12, 1973, it would have been in the area that suffered the most damage in the fire on that date and may have been destroyed. The fire destroyed the major portion of records of Army military personnel for the period 1912 through 1959, and records of Air Force personnel with surnames Hubbard through Z for the period 1947 through 1963. Fortunately, there are alternate records sources that often contain information which can be used to reconstruct service record data lost in the fire; however, complete records cannot be reconstructed.

We are pleased to enclose NA Form 13038, *Certification of Military Service*. This document verifies military service and may be used for any official purpose. A seal has been affixed to this document to attest to its authenticity. The information used to prepare the enclosed NA Form 13038 was obtained from an alternate record source.

If you have questions or comments regarding this response, you may contact us at 314-801-0800 or by mail at the address shown in the letterhead above. If you contact us, please reference the Request Number listed above. If you are a veteran, or a deceased veteran's next of kin, please consider submitting your future requests online by visiting us at http://vetrecs.archives.gov.

Sincerely,

JAMES KRITSELIS
Archives Technician (5A)

Enclosure(s)

**We Value Our
Veterans' Privacy**
*Let us know if we have
failed to protect it.*

Army of the United States
Honorable Discharge

This is to certify that

GEORGE M BOONE 34 486 876 PRIVATE FIRST CLASS
984TH COMPANY 570TH QUARTERMASTER BATTALION

Army of the United States

is hereby Honorably Discharged from the military
service of the United States of America.

This certificate is awarded as a testimonial of Honest
and Faithful Service to this country.

Given at

Date

SEPARATION CENTER
CAMP SHELBY MISSISSIPPI

12 January 1946

ARCHIE SCRUGGS
MAJOR AUS

ENLISTED RECORD AND REPORT OF SEPARATION HONORABLE DISCHARGE

1. LAST NAME - FIRST NAME - MIDDLE INITIAL	2. ARMY SERIAL NO.	3. GRADE	4. ARM OR SERVICE	5. COMPONENT
BOONE GEORGE M	34 486 876	PFC	QMC	AUS
6. ORGANIZATION	7. DATE OF SEPARATION	8. PLACE OF SEPARATION		
984TH CO 570TH QM BN	12 Jan 46	SEP CEN CP SHELBY MISS		
9. PERMANENT ADDRESS FOR MAILING PURPOSES	10. DATE OF BIRTH	11. PLACE OF BIRTH		
OXFORD LAFAYETTE MISS	31 May 20	MYRTLE MISS		
12. ADDRESS FROM WHICH EMPLOYMENT WILL BE SOUGHT	13. COLOR EYES	14. COLOR HAIR	15. HEIGHT	16. WEIGHT	17. NO. DEPEND.
See 9	Brown	Black	5'7"	147	5
18. RACE	19. MARITAL STATUS	20. U.S. CITIZEN	21. CIVILIAN OCCUPATION AND NO.
WHITE NEGRO OTHER (specify)	SINGLE MARRIED OTHER (specify)	YES NO	FARMHAND GENERAL 3-16.10

MILITARY HISTORY

22. DATE OF INDUCTION	23. DATE OF ENLISTMENT	24. DATE OF ENTRY INTO ACTIVE SERVICE	25. PLACE OF ENTRY INTO SERVICE
		11 Dec 42	CP SHELBY MISS
26. SELECTIVE SERVICE DATA / REGISTERED / LOCAL S.S. BOARD NO. / COUNTY AND STATE		28. COUNTY AND STATE	29. HOME ADDRESS AT TIME OF ENTRY INTO SERVICE
YES NO		LAFAYETTE MISS	See 9
30. MILITARY OCCUPATIONAL SPECIALTY AND NO.	31. MILITARY QUALIFICATION AND DATE		
BLACK SMITH 024	None		
32. BATTLES AND CAMPAIGNS			
NEW GUINEA, SOUTHERN PHILIPPINES			
33. DECORATIONS AND CITATIONS			
ATO MED: APTO MED: PHILIPPINE LIBERATION RIBBON WITH BRONZE STAR: GOOD CONDUCT MED: WORLD WAR II VICTORY MED			
34. WOUNDS RECEIVED IN ACTION			
NONE			

35. LATEST IMMUNIZATION DATES				36. SERVICE OUTSIDE CONTINENTAL U.S. AND RETURN		
SMALLPOX	TYPHOID	TETANUS	OTHER (specify)	DATE OF DEPARTURE	DESTINATION	DATE OF ARRIVAL
Sep 43	Sep 43	Sep 43	CHOL NOV 44	9 Jan 44	APTO	21 Feb 44

37. TOTAL LENGTH OF SERVICE				38. HIGHEST GRADE HELD		DATE OF DEPARTURE	DESTINATION	DATE OF ARRIVAL
CONTINENTAL SERVICE		FOREIGN SERVICE				22 Dec 45	US	4 Jan 46
YEARS	MONTHS	DAYS	YEARS	MONTHS	DAYS	PFC 5		
1	1	10	1	11	26			

39. PRIOR SERVICE
NONE

40. REASON AND AUTHORITY FOR SEPARATION
AR 615-365 CONVN OF GOVT RR1-1 (DEMOBILIZATION)

41. SERVICE SCHOOLS ATTENDED	42. EDUCATION (Years)		
	Grammar	High School	College
NONE	7	0	0

PAY DATA

43. LONGEVITY FOR PAY PURPOSES			44. MUSTERING OUT PAY		45. SOLDIER DEPOSIT	46. TRAVEL PAY	47. TOTAL AMOUNT. NAME OF DISBURSING OFFICER
YEARS	MONTHS	DAYS	TOTAL	THIS PAYMENT			
2	5	1	$300	$100		12.80	W F HALL TECH CAPT FD

INSURANCE NOTICE

IMPORTANT IF PREMIUM IS NOT PAID WHEN DUE OR WITHIN THIRTY-ONE DAYS THEREAFTER, INSURANCE WILL LAPSE. MAKE CHECKS OR MONEY ORDERS PAYABLE TO THE TREASURER OF THE U. S. AND FORWARD TO COLLECTIONS SUBDIVISION, VETERANS ADMINISTRATION, WASHINGTON 25, D. C.

48. KIND OF INSURANCE				49. HOW PAID		50. Effective Date of Allotment Discontinuance	51. Date of Next Premium Due (One month after 50)	52. PREMIUM DUE EACH MONTH	53. INTENTION OF VETERAN TO		
Nat. Serv.	U.S. Govt.	None	Allotment	Direct to V.A.					Continue	Continue Only	Discontinue
X				Y	V.A.	31 Dec 45	31 Jan 46	6.60			X

54.	55. REMARKS (This space for completion of above items or entry of other items specified in W. D. Directives)
(PRINT) RIGHT THUMB PRINT	NO TIME LOST UNDER AW 107
	LAPEL BUTTON ISSUED
	ASR(2 Sep 45) 63

56. SIGNATURE OF PERSON BEING SEPARATED	57. PERSONNEL OFFICER (Type name, grade and organization - signature)
George L. Boone	AVA F LEATHERMAN
	1ST LT WAC

STATE OF MISSISSIPPI........Lafayette........County,

This instrument was filed for record on the....18....day of....Sept...., 19..46..at....10....o'clock....a m.,

and duly recorded in Book....4...., page....203....of the....discharge....Records in this office.

....Louis Stephens...., Clerk.

By....................................., Deputy.

WD AGO FORM 53-55
1 November 1944

This form supersedes all previous editions of
WD AGO Forms 53 and 55 for enlisted persons
entitled to an Honorable Discharge, which
will not be used after receipt of this revision.

Army of the United States

Honorable Discharge

This is to certify that

GEORGE M BOONE 34 486 876 PRIVATE FIRST CLASS
984TH COMPANY 570TH QUARTERMASTER BATTALION

Army of the United States

is hereby Honorably Discharged from the military service of the United States of America.

This certificate is awarded as a testimonial of Honest and Faithful Service to this country.

Given at
SEPARATION CENTER
CAMP SHELBY MISSISSIPPI

Date
12 JANUARY 1946

ARCHIE SORENSON
MAJOR AUS

Sometimes I think many of the things that happened to me in my childhood day, God had a purpose in it to help me to be able to go where we are today - through the many things as I went through hard times and all of that.

MARRIAGE LICENSE

STATE OF MISSISSIPPI

MARRIAGE LICENSE

COUNTY OF LAFAYETTE

To any Judge, Minister, Justice or any other Person Lawfully authorized to celebrate the Rites of Matrimony.

YOU ARE HEREBY LICENSED TO CELEBRATE THE **RITES OF MATRIMONY** BETWEEN **MR. GEORGE M. BOONE** and **MISS MAE DEE LOCKHART** and for so doing this shall be your warrant given under my hand and official seal this the **10th** day of **August** in the year of our Lord **One Thousand Nine Hundred** and **Forty-Six**

Mrs. V.H. McElreath   Circuit Clerk
By Rev. J.S. Lowe   D.C.

THE STATE OF MISSISSIPPI,   BY VIRTUE OF A LICENSE

LAFAYETTE COUNTY   _____

FROM THE CLERK OF THE CIRCUIT COURT OF SAID COUNTY OF **LAFAYETTE** I HAVE THIS DAY CELEBRATED THE RITES OF MATRIMONY BETWEEN

MR. GEORGE M. BOONE and
MISS MAE DEE LOCKHART

GIVEN UNDER MY HAND THIS THE **25TH** DAY OF **AUGUST AD 1946**

REV. J.S. LOWE (SEAL)

BARBER RENEWAL LICENSE

WILLIAM G. MILLIKEN
GOVERNOR

STATE OF MICHIGAN
DEPARTMENT OF LICENSING AND REGULATION

BARBER RENEWAL LICENSE

ISSUED BY THE BOARD OF EXAMINERS OF BARBERS

ATTACH
PHOTOGRAPH
HERE

GEORGE M BOONE
26798 SUMPTER RD
BELLEVILLE MI
48111

THIS DOCUMENT IS DULY IS-
SUED UNDER THE LAWS OF
THE STATE OF MICHIGAN.

PERM. I.D. NO.	EXPIRATION DATE	AUDIT NO.
10739	9/30/79	401236

MUST BE DISPLAYED IN A CONSPICUOUS PLACE

BOARD OF BARBER EXAMINERS

LLC-300 (9-92)

M172771   028

YOUR LICENSE MUST BE DISPLAYED IN A PROMINENT PLACE. REVERSE SIDE OF LICENSE CONTAINS IMPORTANT INFORMATION.

JOHN ENGLER
GOVERNOR

STATE OF MICHIGAN
DEPARTMENT OF COMMERCE

H 878394

BOARD OF BARBER EXAMINERS

BARBER
LICENSE

GEORGE M BOONE
26798 SUMPTER RD
BELLEVILLE   MI   48111

PERMANENT I.D. NO.
1701010739

EXPIRATION DATE
09/30/97

3259961

THIS DOCUMENT IS DULY
ISSUED UNDER THE LAWS OF
THE STATE OF MICHIGAN.

TRIBUTE FROM NEW LIBERTY APOSTOLIC FAITH CHURCH

TO
BISHOP G.M. BOONE, D.D.

Thank you Bishop Boone for being our leader, our pastor, our shepherd.

For 50 years you have preached God's messages and taught us God's word so that we can hear what *Thus Saith The Lord!* You stood in the pool and baptized many souls in the Name Of The Lord Jesus Christ then tarried with them until they were filled with the precious gift of the Holy Spirit. But you did not stop there.

You have counseled and married us, provided financial support, blessed our babies, prayed for and visited the sick, buried those whom the Lord called home. But you did not stop there.

You saw to it from the beginning that New Liberty has what we need to be an effective church in the City of Detroit that does more than have service on Sundays. You established several auxiliaries, departments and groups to serve the church so that we all have a role in winning souls for Christ. You ordained and taught ministers, evangelists, deacons and leaders. You taught those who are part of the bus ministry to serve God's people wherever they went. You established the food pantry and the radio ministry to serve the community outside of the church walls. But you did not stop there.

You are yet the example of what we need to be, do, say, and live in order to be the ones God wants us to be. We are proud to call you our Founder. We are honored that you call us your congregation.

The New Liberty Apostolic Church Family

TRIBUTE FROM THE APOSTOLIC ASSEMBLIES OF CHRIST, INC.
TO
BISHOP G.M. BOONE, D.D.

To our honorable and beloved Founder, Bishop G.M. Boone -We would like to take just a moment to say THANK-YOU for your leadership, direction, and vision for our great organization (The Apostolic Assemblies of Christ). We will briefly highlight what these three critical success factors have meant to us:

LEADERSHIP
* You've stood on your watch in the midst of some who has watered down the Apostolic doctrine.
* You've assembled great men and women of God whom you've nurtured and groomed into MEN AND WOMEN OF STANDARD! We are by-product of YOUR leadership.
* You've led by example through your morals, values, and integrity.
* You've given of yourself, your resources, your time, your energy, and your effort - for which, we give you a collective THANK YOU!

DIRECTION
* God has sustained and guided you in leading our organization some 42 years! And Bishop, in the words of the Apostle Paul - "You've fought a good fight, you've finished your course..."! Through numerous NO's you encountered along the way, the Lord planted a YES in your spirit and has rewarded you accordingly!
* We may never know exactly how many churches you've helped establish over the years through your travels, your work as a missionary/evangelist/shepherd and father-figure in the Lord.

VISION
* Without a vision, the people perish. Nevertheless, you've stood in the gap and provided spiritual navigation to countless churches, pastors, and organizations.
* You established a selfless organizational theme - "Everybody is Somebody". Through this simple, yet powerful theme, it has modeled our ministry, our personal philosophy, and built spiritual character within the Apostolic Assemblies of Christ body.

Written by:
Bishop Bramlett Cooper
Memphis, Tennessee

TRIBUTE FROM SHIRLEY ANN MOORE

Daddy, Thanks for the Memories...

Time will not permit me to thank you enough for how you have been there for me all of my life.

As I reflect on the countless memories I've been blessed to share as your daughter, I must say thank you for at least several highlights.

Thank you for ensuring that my childhood was truly a special one. As busy as you were and as involved as you were helping others, you never failed to take time out for your family. I will always cherish the trips you took us on down south to be with my Grandparents and family. I will never forget how we never went without because you were an excellent provider. Your work ethic made it so that we never experienced bill collectors calling our home or not having enough food for the family. Even as a young child, I knew that you were the perfect example of what a real Man is.

How could I forget the night when you anointed my hands and told me at 12 years old that I was going to be your next musician even though I had no training or ability and just a few months later, it came to pass.
Watching you labor to build New Liberty while I was a young child will forever stand out in my mind, but I must also thank you for the memories that were created while building the Apostolic Assemblies of Christ.
You allowed me to travel with you and while it was a lot of work, you always made sure it was also a lot of fun.

After I got married you had a vision in my backyard that I had three children, two boys and a girl and the girl would be the lightest one.
Needless to say, you were right again. Thanks for the Memories.
You are my Hero!

I love you so much! Your Baby Girl

Thanks for the Memories

A TRIBUTE TO DR. GEORGE MARSHALL BOONE

THIS MAN

This man is an **HONORABLE** man, worthy of the praise
He stands for **RIGHTEOUSNESS** in these last and evil days
This man holds the standards of **HOLINESS** up so very high
He teaches the **DOCTRINE** of Christ without compromise
This man is **PASSIONATE** — he has traveled both near and far
He seems to spare no expense to **SERVE** the people of God
This man has the **HEART** and spirit of an angel
He will **TALK** to anyone and seldom meets a stranger
This man is a people person who is always the **SAME**
He can shake a hundred **HANDS** and barely forgets a name
This man has **TOUCHED** souls in many parts of the world
He is God's **JEWEL** among us draped in precious love
This man has fought for a long time to keep **FAITH** and hope strong
He now leaves a **LEGACY** for us to carry on
This man has **TAUGHT** many of us how to walk and live right
He is the founding **FATHER** of the Apostolic Assemblies of Christ
This man we come to pin on our **FLOWERS**
He is certainly **WORTHY** of this present hour
This man in our **HEARTS** we have all made room
He is our **FOUNDER** Dr. George Marshall Boone

We Honor and Adore You!

BISHOP W.T. WALTON & FIRST LADY EVG. GENEVA WALTON

Abundant Life Apostolic Church, Carthage, MS
Southern District Council, Apostolic Assemblies of Christ, Inc.

ABUNDANT LIFE APOSTOLIC CHURCH
807 Martin Luther King Drive • Carthage, MS 39051 • 601-298-0700
Services: SUNDAY 10:30AM • WEDNESDAY 7:30PM • FRIDAY 7:30PM

"God Is Love And Love Is For Everybody"

"Thanks for the Memories"

Things I remember the most I embrace the journey with Bishop G.M. Boone, D.D. Founder of the Apostolic Assemblies of Christ, Inc. The late Bishop George Mickens and our family began our journey in 1978 at the Christ Temple Church under the leadership of the late Bishop Fred Majors and Mother Clara Majors. Where we found the Apostolic Doctrine preached and practiced. The late Bishop George Mickens was a local minister who was very Vigilant and pulsating preacher full of life, zeal and vision. His calling in the 5 Fold Ministry was that of the Pastorate Service.

We served faithfully at the Church in many area's of ministry. After five years, opportunity came to Bishop Mickens from General Motors to take an early retirement with cash-out Benefit. This was a giant step to take because God had given him and I the Vision of going to Hattiesburg, Mississippi. Remembering the word which said, "In the multitude of Council there is safety." We believed that the vision would be confirmed by the Man of God. Bishop Mickens carefully sought after the severance guidance of our Presiding Bishop Boone for advice.

Our future was laid in the hands of the Lord; we believed in his ability to hear the Lord's voice coming from Him. Now here stands the little lady determined to do the right thing and give 100% support to my husband at Bishop Boone's word. I was very persistent in hearing what God would say about it. My spirit and attitude jumped out of my inner man through my eyes "Please let God lead you Bishop Boone, because I don't want to go to Mississippi on a mistake", giving up too much for that!

Bishop Boone's Wisdom, observed the passionate serene spirit of expectation coming at him. And as he always admits he said, "I had to hear from God," and just as his relationship with God proves him to be the Anointed man who hears from God. We were at peace because of the Confidence which we had in our man of God. The evidence yet remains that this move was God's will. From 1978-1996, Bishop Boone, The Boone family, Church family and the entire Organization has been an un-separated family to the Mickens Family.

In 1996 the all wise God saw it pleasing to remove Bishop Mickens from us and heaven was gain for him. He was a loyal member of the A.A. of C. and wholeheartedly paid his dues with joyful and faithful. He rendered 100% participation to the glory of God. With no life or burial insurance. His sudden death caught us unprepared. Bishop Mickens comically expressed his mind like "When I die, wrap me up in a sheet throw me in a hole behind the Church".

It was about to be that way until the Spirit of love, compassion and sympathy came upon our Bishop and his ability to hear and follow God's word by faith became very apparent.

By the words spoken to our Bishop's Board, Auxiliaries, Leaders everyone complied and, they extended an abundance of support. This great man of God and our A.A. of C. Family came to our side in every way possible. Dr. Moore and Bishop William Harris, IV resided in our home for many days, Our family showed outstanding support and compassion, more than we could have asked for. If our Bishop cannot help you he won't hurt you. Bishop Boone's years, wisdom and love which you showed will never be forgotten. This family will forever have a special place in our hearts for the love and fervent in Spirit you displayed toward The Mickens Family: George & Martha, Tony Sr. & Peggy; Nichole, Tony, Jr., Terrell, Tamar, Takia, Talia, and Tirese; Tasha & Mitchell Sheldon and their son Mitchell Jr., Terry Sr. & Keyona and their family Terry Jr., Torry, Kyra, and Tradjon. And as young Brother T.J. Mickens always exalts and encourages you to "Keep the organization Strong". Our hands are raised in praise for Our Founder Bishop G.M. Boone.

Your Spiritual Daughter, **National Evangelist Martha Cohens**

Thanks for the Memories...

That the aged men be sober, grave, temperate, sound in faith, in charity, in patience. Titus 2:2
Praise the name of Jesus...
<u>**To the Founder of the Apostolic Assemblies of Christ, Inc., Bishop G. M. Boone, D. D.**</u>

I met Bishop Boone in 1985 at a time of great change in my live. We had recently left the Pentecostal Assemblies of the World, and my Pastor, Bishop Casper Cohens, Sr. had since begun Emmanuel Apostolic Faith Church in Greenville, South Carolina.

Upon meeting this distinguished, humble, and gentle giant, I felt as if I had known him all of my life. In hindsight, it was as if he had been waiting for me. He spoke kindly to my Pastor, Bishop Cohens, and to the saints, and thank God, a longtime spiritual relationship with Bishop Boone, Mother Boone, and the Apostolic Assemblies of Christ began...

It was the same year as we were preparing for a special Appreciation Service for our Pastor Bishop Cohens. We invited Bishop Boone to stay in our home for a couple of days while in Greenville, South Carolina. We remember Bishop Boone's kindness, and his way of making us feel at ease, he was the Presiding Bishop, spending a couple of days with us! We were so humbled and honored to have him grace us with his presence. He could have insisted upon having us reserve a room for him at the best hotel in town, but he accepted staying with us in our home. We worked very hard to make things comfortable for him during that event. We hope we did well.

The visits Bishop Boone made to our councils, and special council events gave us an even greater look at this man of God. His wisdom, gracefulness, and shared life experiences, has been of great comfort, and a blessing to all of us, as he imparted to us during those times.

The many Apostolic Assemblies of Christ Semi Annual and National Meetings have been life changing. We remember how Bishop Boone energetically continues to praise God and preaches the Word of God. We remember that after the services, Bishop Boone is known to make great effort to connect with each member, great and small. A man with great personality and know-how has made each member feel as if they were equally important to him, as well as the national body.

Before I became Bishop, you ordained me Deacon. All of my elevations have come through your leadership.

I also remember...how Bishop Boone & Mother Boone, along with others made a great sacrifice to come from Birmingham, Alabama to Inman, South Carolina to help us memorialize our beloved Pastor, Bishop Casper Cohens, Sr. D. Min. The words of comfort Bishop Boone spoke in behalf of our Pastor that day touched the hearts of Mother Cohens, our family, Church family, and friends. We will never forget...

Thanks for the memories... Bishop Boone. You and Mother Boone have been a great influence in my life. I will never forget....

I wouldn't take a <u>**Gold Guinea**</u> for you! (Smile)

Love,

Bishop Johnny L. Davis

Thanks for the Memories

Sometimes in life we will meet someone that has left an indelible mark on us as human beings, for various reasons, whether they be a political figure, an accomplish musician or artist, an athlete, poet or just someone that has made name recognition through some extraordinary feat.

Valor, I would like to write about a **Man of Valor** that may not be regarded as society considered as a decorated symbol. I am speaking of A Man Of God, a legendary figure that God has blessed and given him the wisdom, the strength, longevity and the firmness of God's word that he stands on and maintains today.

This man has left an indelible mark on many lives that he has touched, and or has crossed paths. An iconic figure that's heavily decorated spiritually, not by what society regards as decorated status, but by biblical qualities and standards, the status of fruits and works and that`s what count.

This true statesman I am referring to is non other than the Honorable Bishop George Marshall Boone, someone who has been apart of my life for sometime.

He is a gentle giant, a Rembrandt of qualities, a figure who has courageously and humbly hurdled obstacles, that he continues to fight the good fight of faith.

He has endured multiple heart aches, hardship, disappointments, and even some agonies of defeat in several instances. Even has looked in the eyes of death, he has persevered in spite of it all, this marks a true Man of Valor. Bishop Boone has been there for me as I begin to grow into a young lady, he was very instrumental in my life. He incited wisdom and knowledge within me, he always gave wholesome words and helpful instructions to me and my siblings.

We hold those same sentiments today, but moreover he is still the great man of God that is clothed in wisdom and understanding that you would like to glean from. **"Thanks For The Memories" Bishop Boone.**

As I fast forward through several years and time, I can say that Bishop Boone help sculpture my life both spiritual and naturally, even grooming me to be a great Missionary for now and the future.

I say thank you for the minute, the small, and the very large nuggets that was whittle off of the wood of wisdom from you unto me. The spiritual words that he has deposited into me, I`m so grateful.

Bishop Boone was also a shoulder to lean on in a critical time in my marriage, with prayer, advice and counsel. I can say so much in regards to the help of counsel that was favored and offered within my marriage by him.

Time nor space, will not permit me to record all of the helpful and wholesome advice that was rendered unto me. But I will give a snippet and condense this particular incident that Bishop Boone played a major role in. After I was put out, locked out, and the locks on the doors of my home were changed.

Living in a hotel for fifteen months, Bishop Boone wore this problem very close to his heart. He continued to pray with me for God to move on my behalf, and that God's will be made manifest.

Bishop Boone called me from his home in Belleville, Michigan during this dilemma about 1:00 a.m. Central time, 2:00 a.m. Eastern time. He states that the Lord had awakened him early in the midnight hours (2:00 a.m.) concerning me, his niece and the ordeal and trouble she was facing.

Bishop Boone left this voicemail message on my phone, of all the Lord had given him as the messenger to give me. He spoke with diligent and candor.

He spoke with words of profoundness and solitude, the solitude was to me as being in a lonely place, being put out of my own home, but yet being blanketed by the Holy Ghost, that was the comfort. Bishop Boone spoke on the voicemail as if he was speaking directly to me, very lengthy, you couldn't help but know it was of the Lord. No doubt in my mind, I know God orchestrated this and Bishop Boone was the willing vessel, My, My, what a God we serve. He stated the Lord let him know it wouldn't be that much longer and for me to hold on, be of good cheer, stay encouraged, my deliverance draweth nigh.

These were just words of life and with much anointing, I can't even explain his words of worth...as he talked and talked and talked and he then ended his conversation, with these words, Your Uncle George Loves you, hold on niece it won't be that much longer, quote and now I'm going to go back to sleep, Good Bye and Bye-Bye in quote. The tears flow now as I write, My God what a messenger. God always has a word through His messengers or from Himself.

Thanks For The Memories Bishop G.M. Boone.
Your Favorite Niece, Missionary Sandra Y. Anderson

Reflections

A LEGACY TO BEHOLD...

95TH

BIRTHDAY
Celebration

THIS IS MY STORY

My Mary

69 Years of Marriage

Whoso findeth a wife findeth a good thing,
and obtaineth favour of the Lord.

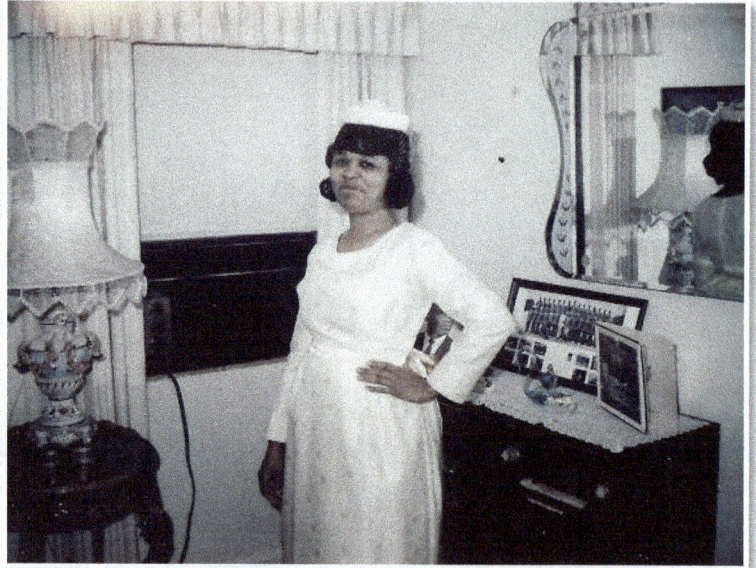

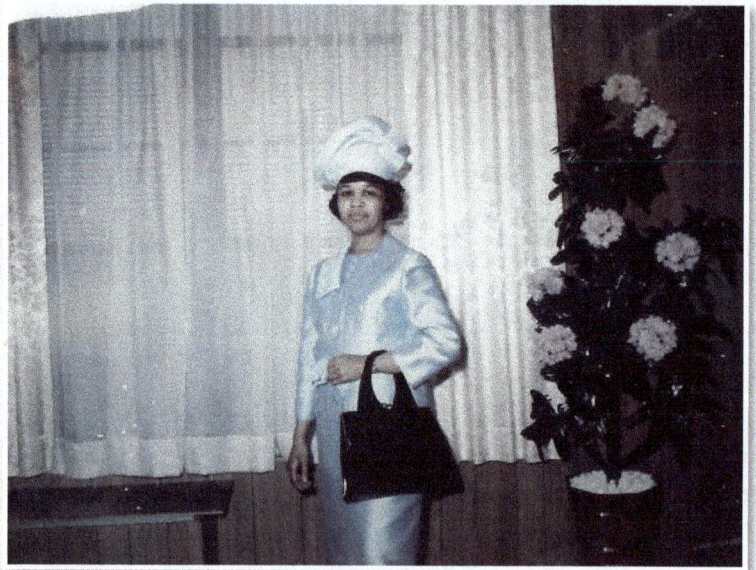

The Mother of My Six Children.

Her children arise up, and call her blessed...

...her husband also, and he praiseth her.

Many daughters have done virtuously,
but thou excellest them all.

MY WIFE - MY PATRON IN THE MINISTRY

Give her of the fruit of her hands;
and let her own works praise her in the gates.

My Wife - My Patron in the Ministry

We work together to maintain our home and family.
She worked just as hard inside the house as I did outside.

Most of all, my labor has not been in vain for the love of my life, my jewel, my business partner, my home partner, my prayer partner, my best friend, my loving, devoted, committed wife, Mae Dee Boone. She worked beside me, raised the children, kept the books, kept appointments and kept the house. Now that she has come to the real golden years of her life where she can reflect on what God has done, He has given us miracle after miracle. She no longer has to keep the books and write out the bills and drive from place to place. God has given her committed, trustworthy people who keep the books, the house, appointments, and drive her everywhere she wants to go.

It is something I will never forget to leave the Lord out.
Any good thing that happens that way,
I have always found a way to say Lord I Thank You!

BISHOP G.M. BOONE, D.D. **169**

69 YEARS OF MARRIAGE

6 Children, 14 Grandchildren &
25 Great-Grandchildren.

THIS IS MY STORY

A Beautiful Journey with my Wife as the Founders of the
New Liberty Apostolic Faith Church
of the
Apostolic Assemblies of Christ, Inc.

We were blessed to serve for 51 years

Having therefore obtained help of God, we continue unto this day...
Acts 26:22

Great Is Thy Faithfulness

I must work the works of him that sent me, while it is day:
the night cometh, when no man can work.

And let us not be weary in well doing:
for in due season we shall reap, if we faint not.

...For I have not shunned to declare unto you
all the counsel of God.

For by me thy days shall be multiplied,
and the years of thy life shall be increased.

A Good Wife by my side

There is a way of making it through the hard times if you put your trust in God.

We are still Standing

As we looked out for the lives of God's people,
now people are looking out for our lives,
my family, my church and the organization.

THIS IS MY STORY

A Beautiful Journey with my Wife as the Founders of the
Apostolic Assemblies of Christ, Inc.

We were blessed to serve for 42 years

Having therefore obtained help of God, we continue unto this day...
Acts 26:22

By the Grace of my Lord, we come along way.

STILL STANDING

For I am persuaded, that neither death, nor life, nor angels, nor principalities, nor powers, nor things present, nor things to come, Nor height, nor depth, nor any other creature, shall be able to separate us from the love of God, which is in Christ Jesus our Lord.

Set the Lord before you and don't be moved.

Stand fast therefore in the liberty wherewith Christ hath made us free, and be not entangled again with the yoke of bondage.

Life is worth living if you allow God to reign in your life.

Life can be Beautiful when God is in it.

APOSTOLIC ASSEMBLIES OF CHRIST PASTORS

that have been with me for over 30 years...

Bishop Sorrells

Bishop Carter

Bishop Newman

Bishop Williams

Pastor Grant

Pastor DuBoise

Bishop Mitchell

Bishop Walton

Bishop Cohens

Bishop Clay

Bishop Davis

SOME OF MY BISHOPS

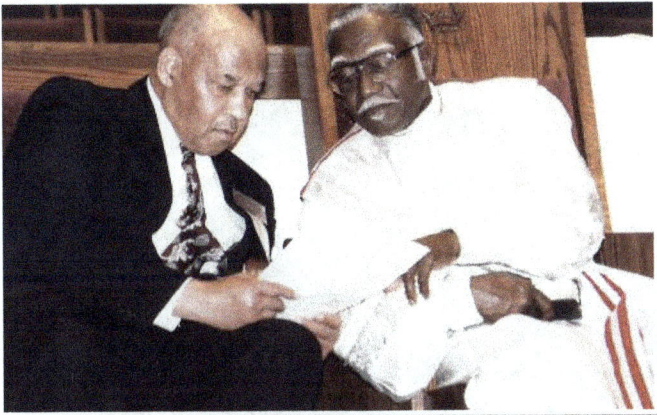
Bishop Oates

Bishop McDowell, Bishop Jones & Bishop Sorrells

Bishop Jordan

Bishop Newman

Bishop Brown

*Bishop Davis, Bishop Cohens,
Jur. Bishop Whaley, Bishop Mitchell, Bishop Cooper
& Bishop Mahone*

My Successors

When I passed the Mantle to my organization and my church,
I knew I was in the will of God.

New Liberty Apostolic Faith Church

Orientation for Impartation - February 19, 2014

Passing of the Mantle - January 11, 2015

*Presiding Bishop Charles H. Ellis, III & Bishop Alfred Singleton
celebrated with me along with many others.*

In March of 1970, the Lord led me to organize the
Apostolic Assemblies of Christ and with His help; I was blessed to serve this great
organization as the Presiding Bishop from 1970 to 2012.
Because of those 42 years of service, the Apostolic World Christian Fellowship
honored me with the distinction of being the longest served
Presiding Bishop in the history of the Apostolic Movement.

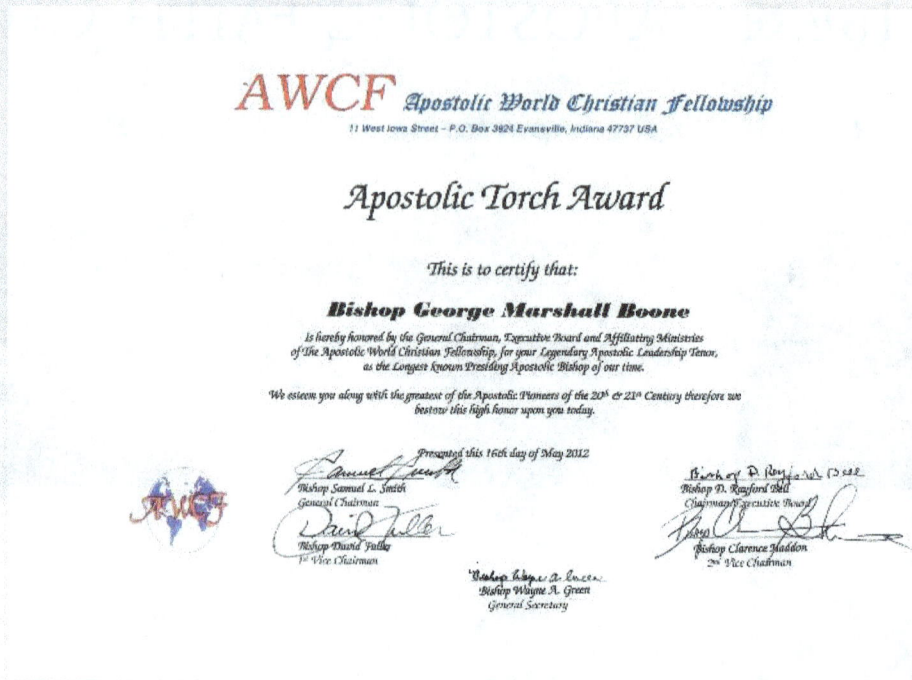

Just as I heard The Lord when He instructed me to found the organization,
I also heard Him when He instructed me to pass the mantle of leadership to my
successor, Bishop Donald Sorrells. On July 27, 2012 at our 42nd National
Convention, I anointed Bishop Sorrells to lead this great movement forward.

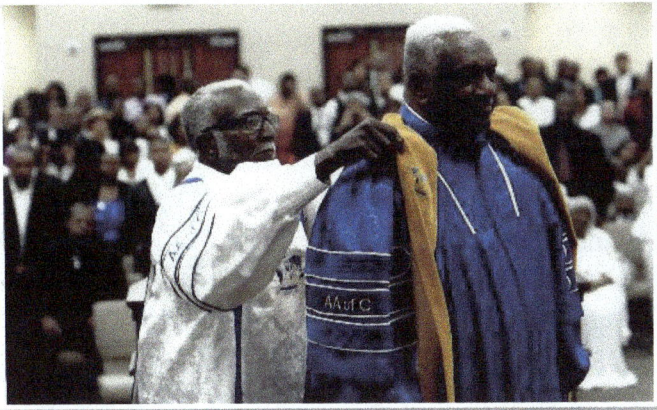

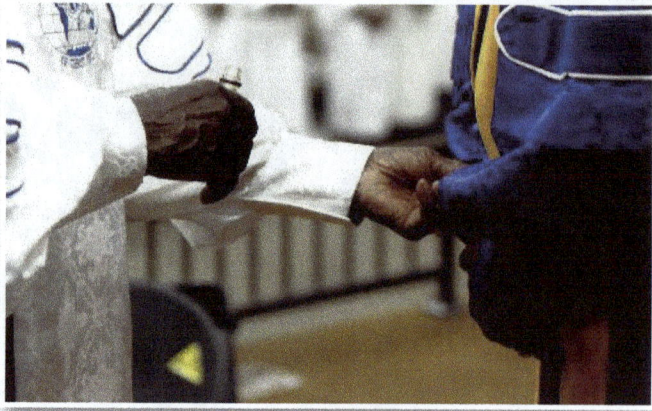

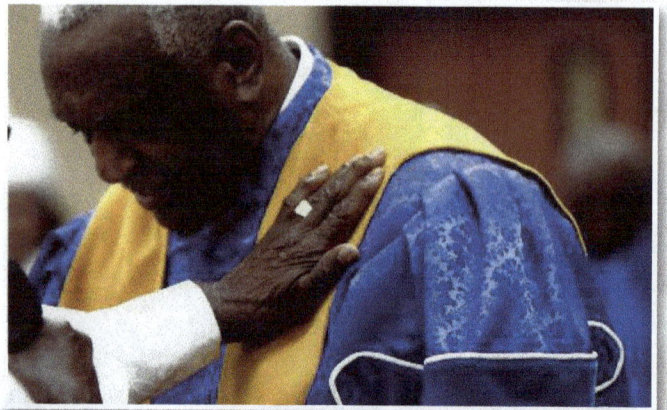

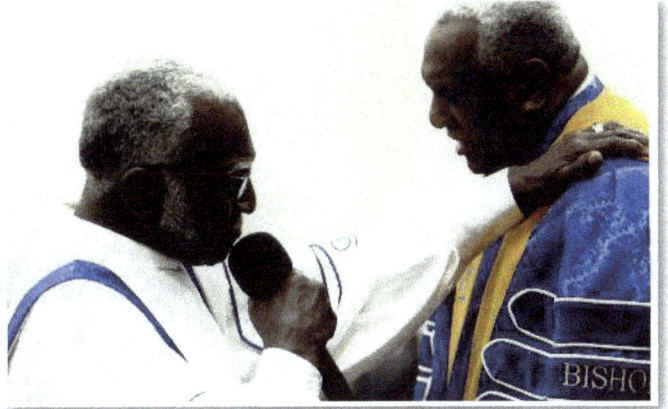

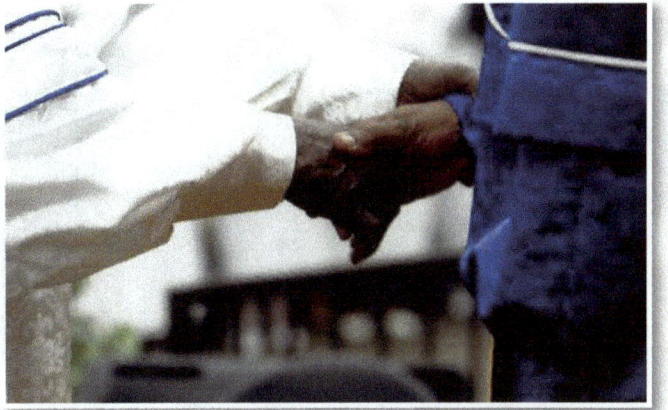

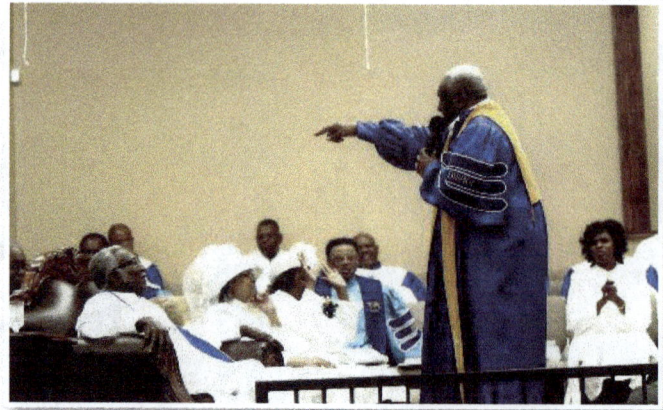

My labor has not been in vain for the
Apostolic Assemblies of Christ.

I Passed the Mantle

At the
ZION UPPER ROOM APOSTOLIC FAITH
365 N. Blakemore Avenue
Gallatin, Tennessee 37066
Bishop Isaac Williams, D. Min. - *Pastor*

Bishop Williams & Myself

WE ARE THE LONGEST SERVED
PRESIDING BISHOP & FIRST LADY
IN THE APOSTOLIC MOVEMENT

Look at God!

The most important thing to me at this stage in my life is that my legacy will be upheld, continued and built upon for the next generations, according to the Divine Will of God.

MARY, WE HAVE WALKED TOGETHER...

69 Years of Marriage
51 Years of Pastoring
42 Years Serving our Organization

Thank you!

It warms my heart and fills my spirit with joy when I see that through my labor and everything I have done, God has brought me to a place where we no longer have to worry about some of the day to day operations of life. God has given me what He gave Moses. Help when I needed it most. But Moses' hands were heavy; and they took a stone, and put it under him, and he sat thereon; and Aaron and Hur stayed up his hands, the one on the one side, and the other on the other side; and his hands were steady until the going down of the sun.

Exodus 17:12

SPECIAL THANK YOU

My Daughter, Dr. Shirley Ann Moore

My Editor, Dr. Dorma Jeane McGruder

The Designer, Mrs. Chiquitta Harris

My Grandson, Elder Mark A. Moore, Jr.

My Grandson, Trustee Anthony Boone

My Great Grand Son, Brother Ramone Alvin

First Lady Christine H. Clay & Minister Pamela Williams

My Niece, Mrs. Susan Cooper Perez

My Sister, Mother Dorothy Hampton,

for providing much vital information in this book
before her passing.

EPILOGUE

After reading this book, my prayer is that it is abundantly clear that I am excited about pleasing God. Yes, have heard so much about heaven, but I want to see it for myself. Yes, I've heard about God and walked with Him for decades, but I have to see Him for myself. In fact, even at 95 years old, I want to see what else He has in store for me.

After all that I have seen over my life, I am more convinced now than ever that God can do anything. If we can only get ourselves in the right position to ask Him with the right level of faith, He will do it. The reason that I am so convinced of this is because I am a living witness that He can do anything but fail.

God bless you and join me as we all continue in this great walk of salvation!

THIS IS MY STORY

With all of these things, I feel like now that I have told about the farm, family, army, wife, children, preaching, pastoring, founding a church and an organization, I can say,

I am completely in the Will of God.

I can now say, This Is My Story.

www.ingramcontent.com/pod-product-compliance
Lightning Source LLC
Chambersburg PA
CBHW050416110426
42812CB00006BA/1905